Barnabas for Children® is a registered word mark and the logo is a registered device mark of The Bible Reading Fellowship.

Text copyright © The Consultative Group on Ministry among Children 2006, 2013
Illustrations copyright © Peter Stephenson 2006
The authors assert the moral right
to be identified as the authors of this work

Published by
The Bible Reading Fellowship
15 The Chambers, Vineyard
Abingdon, OX14 3FE
United Kingdom
Tel: +44 (0)1865 319700
Email: enquiries@brf.org.uk
Website: www.brf.org.uk

BRF is a Registered Charity
ISBN 978 0 85746 118 6
First published 2006
Revised edition published 2013
10 9 8 7 6 5 4 3 2 1 0
All rights reserved

Acknowledgments
Unless otherwise stated, scripture quotations are taken from the Contemporary English Version of the Bible published by HarperCollins Publishers, copyright © 1991, 1992, 1995 American Bible Society.

Scripture quotations taken from the Holy Bible, New International Version, copyright © 1978, 1984, 2011 by Biblica (formerly International Bible Society), are used by permission of Hodder & Stoughton Publishers, an Hachette UK company. All rights reserved. 'NIV' is a registered trademark of Biblica (formerly International Bible Society). UK trademark number 1448790.

Scripture quotations taken from The New Revised Standard Version of the Bible, Anglicized Edition, copyright © 1989, 1995 by the Division of Christian Education of the National Council of the Churches of Christ in the USA, are used by permission. All rights reserved.

Scriptures quoted from the Good News Bible published by The Bible Societies/HarperCollins Publishers Ltd, UK © American Bible Society 1966, 1971, 1976, 1992, used with permission.

A catalogue record for this book is available from the British Library

The paper used in the production of this publication was supplied by mills that source their raw materials from sustainable managed forests. Soy-based inks were used in its printing and the laminate film is biodegradable.

Printed in Singapore by Craft Print International Ltd

Core Skills

FOR CHILDREN'S WORK

Developing and extending key skills for children's ministry

The Consultative Group on Ministry among Children

Core Skills for Children's Work is offered as training material by the Consultative Group of Ministry among Children (CGMC), a network of Churches Together in Britain and Ireland.

Churches and organisations currently represented on CGMC

ACTS Scotland
Arise Ministries
Baptist Union of Great Britain
BRF
CYM (Centre for Youth Ministry)
Children's Ministry
Christian Education
The Church Lads' and Church Girls' Brigade
Church of England
Church of Ireland
Church of Scotland
Church in Wales
Congregational Federation
Council for Sunday Schools and Christian Education in Wales
Christian Education Association Scotland
Girls Brigade
Godly Play UK
The Methodist Church in Great Britain
Methodist Church in Ireland
The Moravian Church
Presbyterian Church of Wales
Quaker Life
Roman Catholic Church
Roots for Churches
The Salvation Army
Scripture Union
Sunday School Society for Ireland
St Mary's at Gylndwr University
United Reformed Church
International Christian College

Acknowledgments

CGMC wishes to thank all those involved with the project, either with the writing or the field-testing of material, and is grateful for their ideas, inspiration and hard work, which have enabled this publication to evolve from its predecessor, *Kaleidoscope*, into new, exciting and vibrant training material.

Particular thanks go to Rosemary Johnston and Steve Pearce for acting as coordinators for the project, to Roger Walton for guiding the initial steps, and to Sue Doggett and BRF for understanding, encouragement and gentle guidance along the way.

We also extend a special thank you to the Westhill Endowment for their generous support for the writing, launching and ongoing development of the CORE project.

From the writing group

The production of the *Core Skills for Children's Work* (CORE) material has been a creative ecumenical journey.

For some time, a variety of basic courses had been produced to encourage and equip those working with children in the church. Then, through the Consultative Group on Ministry among Children (CGMC), a group was set up to produce the first ecumenical training material. *Kaleidoscope: Training material for those working with children in the church* was published in 1993 and has been hugely successful. More than 15,000 copies have been sold and many more people have enjoyed training locally with others from a wide variety of churches. It has been translated into Welsh, and the Swedish translation was used ecumenically by the Baptist, Methodist and Swedish Mission Covenant Churches in Sweden.

However, there is a growing awareness of changes in the context for children's ministry. Insights about children's spiritual development and learning, as well as exploration of fresh approaches to worship and community participation, have led to the need for new material.

Denominations are now making more overt their expectation that those entrusted with the well-being of children should be appropriately trained. In fact, since this book was first published in 2006, *Core Skills for Children's Work* has been reprinted and is now very widely used across all denominations across the UK; for some, it is their standard course material for all training in children's work. In addition, *More Core Skills for Children's Work* was published in 2010 with six further training modules.

The working group set up by CGMC to enable the first book represented the range of denominations in the membership of Churches Together in Britain and Ireland, with representatives from Wales, Scotland, Ireland and England. From this sprang the principles, aims, objectives, writing groups, editorial meetings, pilot groups and, finally, the completed material.

A year's collaborative work led to the six sessions, alongside their supporting website, and the opportunity to gather a portfolio to give evidence of learning. This original material has now been revised by a new working party from CGMC, which has drawn on wide experience of using the sessions in a number of contexts. A constant thread, however, in both the original writing and the revision process, has been an ecumenical generosity in sharing ideas, time and talent.

Important information

Photocopying permission

The right to photocopy material in *Core Skills for Children's Work* is granted for the pages that contain the photocopying clause: 'Reproduced with permission from *Core Skills for Children's Work* (Barnabas for Children, 2013) www.barnabasinchurches.org.uk', so long as reproduction is for use in a teaching situation by the original purchaser. The right to photocopy material is not granted for anyone other than the original purchaser without written permission from BRF.

The Copyright Licensing Agency (CLA)

If you are resident in the UK and you have a photocopying licence with the Copyright Licensing Agency (CLA), please check the terms of your licence. If your photocopying request falls within the terms of your licence, you may proceed without seeking further permission. If your request exceeds the terms of your CLA licence, please contact the CLA directly with your request. Copyright Licensing Agency, Saffron House, 6–10 Kirby Street, London EC1N 8TS. Tel 020 7400 3100; fax 020 7400 3101; email cla@cla.co.uk; web www.cla.co.uk. The CLA will provide photocoying authorisation and royalty fee information on behalf of BRF.

BRF is a Registered Charity (No. 233280)

Contents

Foreword

Children's ministry is a vital element of the churches' work. As the church seeks to be faithful in its mission, it must also seek to provide for those children in its midst and strive for the best that can be offered. *Core Skills* is another important step forward in ensuring that we offer the best resources and leadership we can to the children with whom we have contact.

It is particularly beneficial that we have common material to encourage local churches in their thinking and action. The benefits of working collaboratively, as we continue to discover, are enormous. Encouraging our children to grow into God's image as they tell stories, share ideas, explore the Bible and seek inspiration from the Holy Spirit is central to these materials.

Since its publication in 2006, *Core Skills for Children's Work* has become a key component for training in children's work for a significant number of the denominations represented by Churches Together in Britain and Ireland. We are therefore delighted to commend this revised edition of *Core Skills* as a tried-and-tested focus for encouraging the development, skills and knowledge of those engaged in ministry with children. As they respond to the ongoing challenge of enabling children to be a full part of the community of the church, we should commit ourselves to the prayerful support of all who work with children.

Bob Fyffe, General Secretary, Churches Together in Britain and Ireland

Introduction

Guiding principles

All children are made in the image of God. They are loved unconditionally by God and were affirmed in the life and ministry of Jesus. This is reflected in the Christian community, where:

- ✤ God's love is made real through human life and relationships.
- ✤ All children and adults are of equal value.
- ✤ The Holy Spirit speaks powerfully through children as well as adults.
- ✤ Everyone experiences enjoyment, safety and encouragement in belonging.
- ✤ All contribute and all receive, learning from each other.
- ✤ The Bible is accessible to all.
- ✤ All respect one another as people of faith.
- ✤ Differences are acknowledged and diversity celebrated.
- ✤ All are being changed by the love of Christ and share the good news in the wider community.
- ✤ Worship, celebration and encountering God are vital to the growth of faith.
- ✤ All have a sense of belonging to the universal Church and of serving the world together.

Rights of the Child

The UN Convention on the Rights of the Child has been an important document for all those working with children, both in and out of the church. Its main drives are reflected through CORE, which are as follows.

- ✤ Calling for the provision of specific resources, skills and contributions necessary to ensure the survival and development of children to their maximum capability.
- ✤ Requiring the creation of means to protect children from neglect, exploitation and abuse.
- ✤ When adults are making decisions that affect children, children have the right to say what they think should happen and have their opinions taken into account, while recognising that the level of a child's participation in decisions must be appropriate to the child's level of maturity.

Safeguarding and Child Protection

CORE does not include Child Protection training. The majority of denominations in Britain and Ireland have their own policies, procedures and training, to which all participants in CORE should look.

CORE recognises the centrality of Safeguarding and Child Protection to all our work with children, so we recommend that the information sheet on page 14 is completed by all participants before starting CORE. A copy of this sheet can then be included in your portfolio.

CORE aims and learning outcomes

Aim One

To help participants to develop an understanding of children and the skills required to nurture children in their journey of faith.

Learning outcomes

- ✤ To experience and understand the process of how people develop, learn and grow in faith.
- ✤ To listen to and accompany children as partners in faith.
- ✤ To evaluate their own skills, gifts, strengths and weaknesses and identify a plan for personal development.
- ✤ To help children engage with the Bible as a part of the living, personal and ongoing story.
- ✤ To work creatively with children, using a variety of methods to suit different learning styles.
- ✤ To develop skills to encourage children in expressing and valuing their spirituality and making their own response of faith.
- ✤ To share resources and ideas.

Aim Two

To provide the participants with the opportunity to explore and reflect on their own experience of faith and their Christian journey, and the effect it has on their work with children.

Learning outcomes

✤ To recognise the need to feel valued, equipped and supported in their role.
✤ To reflect on and share their own faith story.
✤ To develop a reflective, enquiring approach to the Bible and its use in faith and life.
✤ To explore their experience of worship, celebration and spiritual life.
✤ To recognise the role of, and raise their awareness of, children's ministry.
✤ To develop the skills and habit of reflecting on their work with children.

Aim Three

To help participants capture and share a vision of a Christian community in which children's faith is expressed and valued.

Learning outcomes

✤ To articulate an understanding of God's call to be a pilgrim people, a missionary community and a global family.
✤ To advocate the active participation of children in mission and ministry.
✤ To explore ways of working with children in a variety of contexts, including new expressions of church.

Using CORE

This material is planned for ease of use in a variety of ways. As the material has been written from a number of ecumenical settings, it is hoped that it will be delivered ecumenically wherever possible.

If you are not sure where CORE might be happening or who might be coordinating it, you should contact your national denominational or organisational office or contact CGMC through the website www.cgmcontheweb.com.

Each of the six sessions is designed to stand alone. It would make sense to do them in the order suggested, but it is possible for an individual or group to select one session and then perhaps add others at a future date. This could happen occasionally over time; alternatively, all the sessions could be tackled in a regular pattern of one per week, fortnight or month. Once a week would give less time for reflection and putting ideas into practice, so a longer gap is recommended. A wider spread of time gives the opportunity to add visits to places of interest as well as exploring the web links.

Each session is designed to take two hours. This timespan will be achieved by selecting from the material available. Each session could be extended to cover a whole day by using more of the material, adding some from the website and slowing the pace in items used, to allow more discussion, exploration and activity. Instead of allotting specific timings to each activity, which will rarely reflect the actual experience of every group using the material, 'apple' indicators have been used instead.

✤ One apple indicates a simple introductory activity that might take only a short time to complete.
✤ Two apples indicate a more in-depth activity that will require some thought and time.
✤ Three apples indicate a high-content section containing the main thrust of the teaching.

By choosing more of the one-apple activities and fewer of the three-apple ones, you will have a shorter session. The reverse, of course, will give a longer session.

A CORE session is laid out as follows.

✤ **Aim** of the whole module.
✤ **Learning outcomes** that should be achieved through the session.
✤ **Materials** needed to run the session.
✤ **Opening thought** to enable reflection.
✤ **Starters:** ways into the topic.
✤ **CORE:** the main teaching element.
✤ **Biblical thought**, tying the teaching to the Bible.
✤ **Reflection on learning:** a prompt to help better understanding of the session.
✤ **Worship:** suggestions to close the session in themed worship.
✤ **Personal reflection sheet** to assist participants in noting their learning outcomes.
✤ **Portfolio checklist** for those wishing to collect evidence of learning.

Resources, including websites, books, and articles, that may be useful for each session are posted on the CGMC website: www.cgmcontheweb.com.

The lists will be added to and updated regularly. Suggestions for inclusion on these lists are always welcome.

The CGMC website is an exciting part of the training. It offers many additions to the book as well as the chance for all to expand their CORE knowledge. Website features include:

- ❖ Contact details for denominations and organisations.
- ❖ Additional CORE modules for sale and download.
- ❖ Resources for trainers, including PowerPoints for each session, logos, downloadable pages from the book and certificates.

The personal reflection sheet can be completed by the participant at home or at the end of the session. It is intended to enable the answering of the following questions.

- ❖ What did you learn from this session?
- ❖ How will this affect the way you work with children?
- ❖ Which items in this area would you like to follow up?

It is possible to obtain academic accreditation for completing *CORE Skills* by undertaking some further written work based on the *CORE Skills* sessions. Full details can be found on the Core Skills website.

Safeguarding and child protection

Title of your denomination's policy document:

What do you do if you have an issue relating to child protection?

Who is the person in your church who deals with child protection issues?

What permission and registration forms do you complete when a new child joins the group?

What training in child protection have you had?

If none, when is the next available training?

When is the next review of your local child protection procedures?

Reproduced with permission from *Core Skills for Children's Work* (Barnabas for Children, 2013) www.barnabasinchurches.org.uk

Introductory session

Aim

To provide a basic introduction to working with children in a church context.

Learning outcomes

- ❖ To share hopes and fears about working with children.
- ❖ To reflect critically on a variety of strategies for developing relationships with children.
- ❖ To evaluate the use of a code of conduct.
- ❖ To explore issues around children, theology and culture.
- ❖ To consider how to approach a session with children.
- ❖ To determine future learning needs.

Materials needed

Before the session
- ❖ Labels or name badges for people as they arrive

Starters
- ❖ Flipchart paper and pens
- ❖ An apple
- ❖ Post-it notes

Core
- ❖ Copies of 'Children and church' questionnaire (see page 20)
- ❖ Copies of 'Assessing training needs' questionnaire (see page 21)

Opening thought

'Are not two sparrows sold for a penny? Yet not one of them will fall to the ground unperceived by your Father. And even the hairs of your head are all counted. So do not be afraid; you are of more value than many sparrows.'
Matthew 10:29–31 (NRSV)

Our role in working among children for the church involves being God's representative in communicating God's love and care. His love and care are also shown to children by the way we act towards each other as adults. In this learning session, the group will not count the hairs on each member's head, but will develop a better understanding of each other's role in children's ministry.

Starters

Who am I?

> **You will need:**
> * Flipchart paper and pens

In threes, check that you know each other's names, then find out about the context of each other's children's work. Talk about:

* How you each feel half an hour before a session begins.
* Your hopes and concerns about working with children and young people.

There will be feedback only on the hopes and concerns, which should be written on flipchart paper.

In the whole group, feed back your hopes and concerns and write them on flipchart paper. Then discuss the hopes and concerns that the children may be bringing to the groups with which the participants are involved. Write them up on the flipchart too, and compare this list with the first.

Think about how to find out how children are really feeling. Why is it important to find out?

Apple consequences

> **You will need:**
> * An apple

Take the apple and start off a story about it: for example, 'This apple came from a small orchard not far from here, and one day...' Pass the apple to someone else in the group, who must continue the story, using the word 'apple' in their contribution to the story. Pass it around the whole group so that everyone contributes, and continue until the story is complete.

Why am I here?

> **You will need:**
> * A flipchart or large sheet of paper, and pens
> * Post-it notes

How many ways can this question be answered? Write as many as you like, one on each Post-it note. It is up to individuals how they interpret the question. Stick the responses on to a flipchart, without comment.

Join up with one or two other people and talk more specifically about why each person is here in this group. Come back into the whole group and talk about the experiences of this activity.

* How did different people interpret the question?
* How did people feel during the Post-it exercise?
* What insights does this exercise give into working with children?

CORE

Children and their culture

Any adult who wants to work with children needs to understand a little about what it is like to be a child in today's world. The way an adult sees the world is quite different from the way a child sees it. An adult leader can never be a child but can make some effort to get inside the world of children.

There are many important and powerful influences on children, and the values that are strongly communicated through the media are significant and formative. Spending time on children's websites, reading magazines aimed at children and exploring current electronic games for children is a good investment and gives pause for thought.

Look at a selection of children's magazines. Skim-read them to get a feel of the impact and tone of the publication. As you read:

* Ask yourself what is the message being given there about school/home/lifestyle/spirituality/young women.
* List any words or phrases you don't recognise.
* Identify one or two articles that you would like to share with the rest of the group.
* Note the main themes of the advertising.

Share your findings with the rest of the group. If there is time together, try putting the values that children observe and experience in the media alongside those communicated explicitly and/or implicitly by the church, and see the differences. Make two lists and ask:

❖ Which culture is easier to understand?
❖ How easy is it to be part of both?
❖ How easy is it to make choices within each culture?
❖ If the church is 'counter cultural', what does that mean?

The world of children and how children develop is explored further in Core Session 1.

Children and church

> You will need:
> ✳ Copies of the 'Children and church' questionnaire (see page 20)

Individually, complete the 'Children and church' questionnaire and then share responses together. How far are these statements true of the church you attend? (Mark 0 for 'Not true at all' and 5 for 'This is clearly our church's belief and practice'.)

Approaching a session

Share the experience of a memorable session you have led with children, one you have seen led, or one you experienced as a child. What worked well and why did you remember it?

What challenges have you met, or are you anticipating, in your work with children? Compile a list of these challenges under the following headings:

❖ Starting a session
❖ Using time in a session
❖ Working with a whole group
❖ Choosing activities
❖ Working with other leaders

The following thoughts may start off your discussion.

Starting a session
Think about how the tone is set in the first five minutes (atmosphere, layout, welcome and so on). How can you start the session off to build relationships with the children?

Using time in a session
When planning, always build in time to engage with a group and individual children. Consider the fact that one-to-one conversation is usually easier when a child is engaged in a practical task, especially a low-key task.

Working with a whole group
Use 'circle time' techniques from time to time. With younger children, a 'show and tell' can be an important, regular part of the session. For older children, frequent positive affirmation games will build up the group's capacity to relate positively and share more deeply.

Choosing activities
Always plan to spend time on what is important, and avoid giving time to activities that benefit the adults more than the children. For example, if you meet on a Sunday morning, avoid a weekly commitment to 'producing' something that has to be performed for the adults in church.

Working with other leaders
Consider how you plan and review together.

Assessing training needs

> You will need:
> ✳ Copies of the 'Assessing training needs' questionnaire (see page 21)

This session has drawn attention to just some of the skills and knowledge that are important for any adult working with children on behalf of the church. Some of this skill comes with experience, but only if you take time to do some conscious learning as well, and also take time to reflect critically on your experiences. Many church denominations have recognised the six sessions of this CORE training as the basic training requirement for children's workers. Look at the outline of these CORE sessions on the 'Assessing training needs' questionnaire and fill in the boxes to help you assess which topics are priorities for you.

Biblical thought

Children and church
Split into three groups, each group looking at one of these Bible passages: Psalm 78:1–8; Matthew 18:1–5; Luke 13:34–35.

If this was the only passage in the Bible you read, what would your 'theology' (your understanding of God's view) of children be? Try to sum it up in three statements, and briefly sum up how this would affect the life of the whole church. What do you feel now about the way you would work with children in your church, and why?

In the whole group, consider the different 'theologies' that different church traditions have, and the different ideas there are about why children are in the church. You may recognise the following models.

❖ If the children are considered to be the church of tomorrow and will only become useful disciples when they become adult members, the provision for children may be aimed at keeping them in contact with the church so that their real learning and work can begin when the time comes.

❖ If the children are seen as the church of tomorrow but need to lead a Christian life now, the children's work may be seen as a schooling in the Christian life. The children's activities may work on the assumption that the faith must be learnt and a Christian way of life followed. Information giving and Bible teaching will aim to lead to a vibrant adult faith and spiritual life.

❖ If children are seen as being as much a part of today's church as the rest of the congregation, and equally valuable members, then it will be vital that children's provision in the church is of a high quality, aimed at equipping their ministry. Children will be enabled to take part in all aspects of church life.

If someone came into your church and tried to guess what your theology of children was by watching the life of the church, what conclusions do you think they would draw? Think about visiting another church and guessing what their theology of children might be.

Reflection on learning

Building relationships with children _____

What are the group's observations of how they have all worked together so far?

Every group has some principles about how the relationships in the group will work—between children, between adults, and between children and adults. Some of those principles will be explicit (having quiet periods to listen to others, keeping each other safe by not running around, and so on) and some implicit (how children address adults, how the children are involved in decision making, and so on).

In a new group, in an established group meeting for the first time after a break, or in a group with lots of new members, it may be good to work together to produce a code of conduct and agree on it. The process for doing this will be important: perhaps there will be some suggestions from both

adults and children, followed by a voting procedure to decide which ones are to be included. Read the following examples and share your responses to them.

Rules set by the leaders
Don't run.
Don't shout.
Don't answer back.
When the leader is talking, listen.
Have fun!

Rules compiled by the children
Welcome to our club. We hope you have a good time, but when you are here you need to do things in our club way. We don't like anyone skittin' people, because we are all friends. Don't bring any sweets or chocolate just for you! We like playing silly games and running round, but when the leaders tell us to stop, we STOP! You'll probably find out that we are all a bit (lot!) noisy and talk too much. But we need to remember that when one of the leaders is telling us what to do, we shut up and listen. And we need to listen to each other as well.

We have one word that is banned—BORING. And we don't use any swear words at all. We have drinks every week so you don't need to bring your own. Finally, at the end of the night, no one goes home until someone comes to pick them up.

We hope you have a good time at our club.

Rules agreed by everyone
Be nice.
Help others.
Respect everybody.
Do the activities when the leaders ask us to.
Make new friends.
Help new people.
Enjoy ourselves.
Listen carefully.
Walk.
Join in.
Don't hit or kick people.
Don't refuse to join in.
Don't be nasty.
Don't run round the room.
Don't talk when someone else is talking.
Don't leave the club room.

How would you go about working with your group to agree a 'code of conduct'?

Worship

Read 1 Corinthians 12:4–6. As a focal point, have a selection of apples used in different ways: apple juice, apple pies, toffee apples and so on. Take time while listening to some music to consider the gifts and talents that you have in relation to children's ministry, because we all have a concern for children and can offer our different skills in different ways. Finish this meditation with a prayer together.

Suggested song

The Lord is good to me
and so I thank the Lord
for giving me the things I need,
the sun and the rain and the apple seed.
The Lord is good to me.

And every seed that grows
will grow into a tree,
and one day soon there will be apples there
for everyone in the world to share.
The Lord is good to me.

'Johnny Appleseed': www.scoutingresources.org.uk/songs/ songs_short.html#johnnyappleseed

At the close of the session, invite everyone to share in the variety of apple products together, in celebration of their involvement in children's ministry.

Children and church questionnaire

Mark 0 for 'Not true at all' and 5 for 'This is clearly our church's belief and practice'.

1.	Children are considered important in our church.	0	1	2	3	4	5
2.	People in our church feel comfortable with children.	0	1	2	3	4	5
3.	Children in our church are happy to be there.	0	1	2	3	4	5
4.	People in our church are willing to support children's work by praying.	0	1	2	3	4	5
5.	People in our church are keen to see children involved in worship throughout the year.	0	1	2	3	4	5
6.	Children are encouraged to join in with other church activities as well as worship.	0	1	2	3	4	5
7.	The adults in our church talk to the children and know their names.	0	1	2	3	4	5
8.	When the children enter the church, they are ignored, but someone greets their parents.	0	1	2	3	4	5
9.	We want children in our church to keep the church going in the future.	0	1	2	3	4	5
10.	There is evidence around the building of the children's involvement in church life.	0	1	2	3	4	5
11.	Our church wants our children to see that God loves them and has a purpose for their lives.	0	1	2	3	4	5
12.	Our church wants children to become active members of the church today.	0	1	2	3	4	5
13.	We want children to be able to look back, later in life, with warm affection at what church meant to them.	0	1	2	3	4	5

Reproduced with permission from *Core Skills for Children's Work* (Barnabas for Children, 2013) **www.barnabasinchurches.org.uk**

Assessing training needs questionnaire

No knowledge: **N**   Some knowledge: **S**   Fully confident: **F**

CORE Session 1: Child development

❖ To understand how children develop physically, emotionally, intellectually, socially, morally and spiritually. ☐

❖ To appreciate the range of learning styles and approaches that there can be within a group. ☐

❖ To reflect on personal experience of life and faith, and the effects of this on ways of working with children. ☐

❖ To consider work with children in the light of some theories of human development. ☐

CORE Session 2: Working as a team

❖ To evaluate current skills, gifts, strengths and weaknesses and identify possibilities for personal development. ☐

❖ To recognise the need to feel valued, equipped and supported in their role. ☐

❖ To develop the skills and habit of reflecting on their work with children. ☐

CORE Session 3: Programme planning

❖ To understand how learning styles in childhood differ, and are influenced by society and culture. ☐

❖ To work creatively with children, using a variety of learning styles. ☐

❖ To plan original sessions and deliver published programmes to meet the needs of children. ☐

❖ To develop the practice of reflecting on and evaluating sessions. ☐

CORE Session 4: Children and community

❖ To reflect on stories from different contexts and distil principles of good practice. ☐

❖ To develop strategies for developing new areas of work with children in a variety of contexts. ☐

❖ To advocate the active participation of children in mission and ministry. ☐

CORE Session 5: Pastoral awareness

❖ To share insights about a variety of pastoral issues. ☐

❖ To explore how power is used in working with children. ☐

❖ To identify issues involved in providing a safe environment, physically, emotionally and spiritually, for children. ☐

CORE Session 6: The Bible and prayer

❖ To explore ways of nurturing the innate spirituality of children. ☐

❖ To gain an understanding of the ways in which Bible stories can enrich prayer and faith development. ☐

❖ To experience a time of prayer and reflection. ☐

❖ To develop an awareness of the different styles of prayer that may be used, both in community worship activities and in personal communication with God. ☐

Reproduced with permission from *Core Skills for Children's Work* (Barnabas for Children, 2013) www.barnabasinchurches.org.uk

CORE SESSION ONE
Child development

Aim

To reflect on and extend understanding of how children develop, and to apply this understanding to interaction with children.

Learning outcomes

❖ To understand how children develop physically, emotionally, intellectually, socially, morally and spiritually.
❖ To appreciate the range of learning styles and approaches that there can be within a group.
❖ To reflect on personal experience of life and faith, and the effects of this experience on our ways of working with children.
❖ To consider work with children in the light of some theories of human development.

Materials needed

Starters

❖ Large sheets of paper and pens
❖ A4 sheets of paper

Core

❖ Large sheets of paper and pens
❖ 'Child development' charts photocopied from pages 28–29
❖ 'Images of faith' sheet photocopied from page 30

Worship

❖ Photographs of children (cut from newspapers and magazines) showing different ages/races/abilities, different contexts, different emotions
❖ A table on which to spread out the pictures so that everyone can move round to look at them

Opening thought

The child Jesus grew. He became strong and wise, and God blessed him.
Luke 2:40

Starters

Then and now

> **You will need:**
> * Two large sheets of paper and at least two pens per group

In groups of three or four, talk about the 'When you were seven' questions below, and collect the answers on one of the large sheets of paper. Enjoy sharing responses.

When you were seven:

1 What was your favourite food?
2 What was your favourite toy or game?
3 What was your favourite story?
4 What was your favourite TV or radio programme?
5 Did you know any Christians?
6 What did you know about Christianity and the Christian faith?
7 Did you feel part of a church? Why/why not?

Now work through the 'Now they are seven' questions below, thinking particularly of the children known to the group members. Record the answers on the other large sheet of paper.

Now they are seven:

1 What foods are popular with seven-year-olds today?
2 What toys and games do they play with?
3 What sorts of stories do they like?
4 What TV programmes are the most popular with this age group?
5 Do the children in your group know any Christians other than you?
6 What do they know about Christianity and the Christian faith?
7 Do they feel part of your church? Why/why not?

Display the completed sheets. Everyone look at the answers of other groups. Are there any surprises? Any shocks? Any challenges? What are the implications of all this for work with children?

Alternatively, you can adapt the questions to relate to different age groups, focusing on five-year-olds or ten-year-olds, for example.

Different approaches

> **You will need:**
> * An A4 sheet of paper for each person

The task is to make a paper cup using only an A4 sheet of paper. After ten minutes, or sooner if everyone has finished or given up, look at the results of everyone's efforts.

❖ How many different designs are there?
❖ Can they all be described as cups?
❖ How did you approach the challenge? (Trial and error? Distant memories of doing it in the past? Copying someone else? Working together?)
❖ Would you have felt more (or less) comfortable if you had been given printed instructions, or if someone had demonstrated how the task should be carried out?
❖ What does this show you about yourself and about each other?
❖ How would the children in your group have approached this challenge?
❖ To what extent does your preferred way of learning affect the way you work with your group?

For more information on learning styles, see CORE Session 3, pages 44–46.

CORE

How children grow and develop

> **You will need:**
> * Large sheets of paper and pens
> * 'Child development' charts, photocopied from pages 28–29

Join up with two or three others who work with the same age group of children that you work with. Picture a child or children of this age. On a large sheet of paper, draw the outline of a child and write on it the main characteristics of the age group. Think about all aspects of a child's being: physical, social, emotional, spiritual and intellectual. When finished, compare and contrast your diagram with the 'Child development' charts.

❖ Do the charts help you to understand better how children develop? Why/why not?
❖ To what extent are they relevant to children with special needs?
❖ What insights has this exercise given into understanding the children you work with?

Every child is an individual. Some are gifted and talented in particular ways. Others have special needs of one sort or another, be they mental, physical or emotional. No two children develop in exactly the same way or at the same rate, and there can be wide variations among children of the same age. The differences in the way children develop raise many questions for children's work, including these:

❖ Which methods and activities are most appropriate for the age range?
❖ To what extent do you use them?
❖ What are the implications for working with a mixed age range?
❖ What are the dangers of expecting too much or too little of the children you work with? Which of these two 'traps' do you find it harder to avoid?

Talk about these questions. What other questions occur to you?

Motivation and needs _____

According to Abraham Maslow, an American psychologist, we all have a range of needs, as illustrated in the diagram below. Our most basic needs are at the bottom. Each layer of needs must be met before the next layer can be attended to. So, for example, a person will not be able to feel that they belong if their physical needs and safety needs have not yet been met. When our needs have been met at one level, we are able to move on to the next. If we have unmet needs at lower levels, we are unlikely to be motivated to learn for learning's sake.

The child psychologist Mia Kellmer Pringle, on the other hand, has identified the following needs as being significant in the development of children and young people.

❖ The need for love and security
❖ The need for new experiences
❖ The need for praise and recognition
❖ The need for responsibility

How do these theories relate to your work with children? To what extent do they help you to understand any problems you have had in working with children?

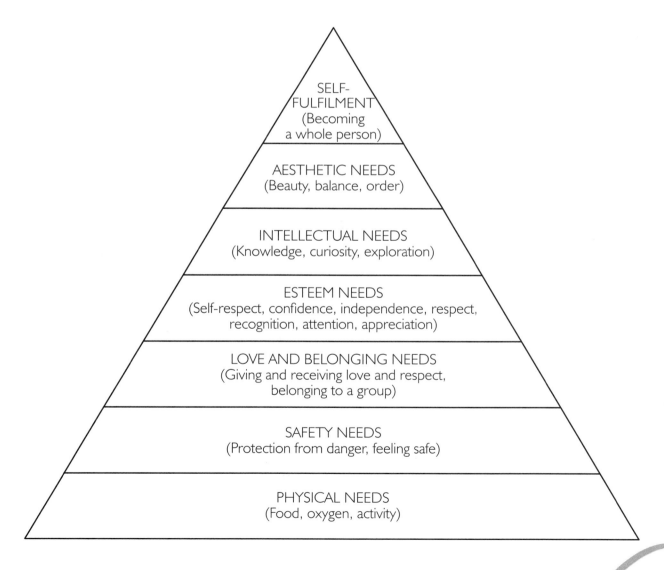

Focus on faith

> You will need:
> * A flipchart or large sheet of paper, pens and pencils
> * 'Images of faith' sheet, photocopied from page 30

Suggest ways to complete the phrase 'Faith is…' For example, could it be said that faith is…

* … a seed to be planted and nurtured?
* … a spring of water needing to be channelled?
* … a quantity of knowledge to be crammed into people's heads?

Look at the 'Images of faith' sheet. Reflect individually on what each image says about faith and the journey through life. Which one 'speaks' most clearly? Is there another image that would illustrate your experience better? If so, draw it in the empty box on the sheet.

Those who wish to share may talk to a partner about why they have chosen a particular image, and in what way it represents their faith journey.

* How does your view of faith affect the way you work with children?
* How does your experience of faith affect the way you work with children?

There are a number of theories on faith development, which can underpin work with children and give a deeper understanding of the process that both children and adults go through in developing their faith. Faith isn't a package to be given to children: it is a process, through which we accompany them.

John Westerhoff, an Episcopal priest, was Professor of Theology and Christian Nurture at the Duke University Divinity School and is a distinguished lecturer, scholar and writer. He developed a theory with a progression through four 'styles of faith', outlined below.

* How do these ideas relate to your own experience of your growth of faith and the faith development of others?
* What are the implications for your work with children?

Westerhoff's faith development theory

* **Experienced faith:** Theological words and doctrines are unimportant. Experiences of trust, love and acceptance provide opportunities for faith to form.

* **Affiliative faith:** Stories, experiences of awe and mystery, feelings and religious experiences combine to give a sense of belonging. There is a strong need to belong, to participate and to identify with the community of faith.
* **Searching faith:** This is a time of questioning, doubting, experimenting with other ideas and finding alternative suggestions and explanations.
* **Owned faith or mature faith:** This is a combination of the affiliative and searching styles of faith. People now want to put their faith into personal and social action, to stand up for what they believe. Owned faith is enriched and developed by the challenge of different perspectives on the truth.

Alister Hardy, a British zoologist, believed that we are 'religious animals' by nature. In surveys and research in the UK, a high proportion of adults say that they have had a spiritual experience at some time in their lives, but few of them have ever talked about it and few are involved in a formal religious institution such as a Christian church.

Read the poem 'A World Prayer', written by a nine-year-old in a school RE lesson.

* Is there anything in the poem that surprises you?
* If we are born naturally religious, why are there not more people of all ages in the churches?

A World Prayer: Hallowed be thy name

Two tall towers,
Like two people hugging,
Praying,
'Hallowed be thy name.'

A meadow of poppies,
Like a river of blood cutting through the world,
Bleeding,
'Hallowed be thy name.'

A football crowd,
A symbol of sport,
Echoing,
'Hallowed be thy name.'

The sticky spring water,
Trickling down the face of a thirsty child,
Laughing,
'Hallowed be thy name.'

A white and black cloud,
A sign of friendship,
Touching,
'Hallowed be thy name.'
© Christian Education

David Hay, a British academic, in his book, *The Spirit of the Child*, says that all children are interested in four fundamental questions:

✤ Who am I?
✤ Where have I come from?
✤ Where am I going?
✤ What am I meant to do?

In order to accompany children on their journey of faith, it is necessary to allow them to explore and articulate their questions. Children need a safe space to explore these questions. As in physical and mental development, it is vital to be aware that children of the same age may not have developed to the same stage or style of faith.

✤ Do you agree that your role is to 'accompany children on their journey of faith'? Why/why not?
✤ How do you encourage children to ask fundamental questions?
✤ How can you enable your children to grow and develop as people of faith?
✤ How can the church avoid making children feel that they should adopt adult religious language and activities rather than expressing their faith in their own ways?
✤ Think about the experiences of worship on offer to the children in your group. Are there any changes you would like to see made in the light of this session?

There are more opportunities to think about prayer and spirituality in CORE Session 6.

Biblical thought

Jesus and children ⎯⎯⎯⎯⎯

Read Mark 9:33–37 and 10:13–16. (Note that in Mark 9:36, the Good News Bible differs from other translations in saying that Jesus placed the child at the front.) What do these passages have to say to us about children's place and the way Jesus saw children?

Jesus placed the child at the centre, where they were part of what was happening—not in front where they would be uncomfortable, not at the back where they would be uninvolved, but in the middle. What steps can you take to prevent the children in your church from feeling either uncomfortable and embarrassed or uninvolved?

There is also an implication that children have a ministry. Share your own experiences of children ministering to others. How can you make it easier for the children in your church to discover and exercise their ministries?

What do you think Jesus meant when he told his disciples to 'receive the kingdom of God like a little child'?

Reflection on learning ⎯⎯

✤ What questions do you have about life and faith? Where do you look for answers?
✤ What do you think a new child would like or need to know about your children's group? Talk to the children in your group about this. What practical things can be done to enable a new child to settle in and want to keep being involved?

Worship ⎯⎯⎯⎯⎯⎯⎯⎯

> You will need:
> ✳ Photographs of children (cut from newspapers and magazines) showing different ages/races/abilities, different contexts, different emotions and so on
> ✳ A table on which to spread out the pictures, so that everyone can move round to see them

Choose one picture that 'speaks' to you. What is this child's life like? What might you want to say to them? What are they saying to you?

Read Mark 9:33–37 and 10:13–16 again, and spend a few moments in silent reflection. Imagine the scene, including the child in the photograph. Bring that child to Jesus in your imagination. Now bring the children in your group to Jesus. What does Jesus say to them? What do they say to him? Where are you in the scene? Do you want to say anything to Jesus? What does he say to you?

Pray (aloud or silently) for the children in your group and for each other.

Suggested songs

Father, I place into your hands (*Songs of Fellowship*, Kingsway)
Moses, I know you're the man (*Partners in Praise*, Stainer and Bell)
One more step along the world I go (*Partners in Praise*, Stainer and Bell)
Take, O take me as I am (*Come All You People*, Wild Goose Publications)

Alternatively, choose a song likely to be known by the whole group, or listen to a piece of music.

Child development

	0–2	3–5	5–7	8–11	12–13	13+
Physical	Rapid physical changes and development Goes from non-mobile to fully mobile Explores the world using all the senses	Runs, skips, jumps Holds a pencil or crayon Cuts with scissors but may need help Peak time for childhood illnesses	Dances, hops Very active; often enjoys climbing/running Fine coordination developing Learning to write Can dress themselves, coping with zips and buttons	May be very involved in sport Kicks and throws balls with accuracy Needs space for active games Practice continues to improve fine coordination Puberty for some girls	Rapid growth May be a large physical difference between girls and boys Puberty May become clumsy	Puberty Boys catch up with girls in growth and development Often unaware of their own strength Capable of activities requiring very fine motor control
Social	Relationships mainly with parents Self-centred Plays next to rather than with others	Begins to develop relationships with other children Cooperates in play Knows own full name Likes consistency in those who are providing care Boundaries very important	Eager to be accepted by peers Beginning to identify themselves as a member of a group May laugh along with a group even if they don't understand what the cause of the laughter is	Close friendships with children of the same sex Identifies with leaders, pop stars and sports stars Learns to lose games gracefully Likes jokes Can be very competitive	Growing ability to put themselves in other's shoes Wider range of friendships Increasing independence from parents Strong loyalty to team and friends Changes in friendship groups First boyfriend or girlfriend	Often conflict with parents Friendships appear to take priority over family relationships Relationships with peers usually very strong May choose a particular style—for example, Goth, skater

Reproduced with permission from *Core Skills for Children's Work* (Barnabas for Children, 2013) www.barnabasinchurches.org.uk

Child development

	0–2	3–5	5–7	8–11	12–13	13+
Mental and intellectual	Explores the world around them; Learning to talk and communicate; Short attention span; Loves bright colours, faces and movement	Communication skills increase; Thinks literally; Asks who, what, why—sometimes with no end; Accepts what adults tell them; Attention span still short	Concrete thinking; Follows simple instructions; Length of concentration increases so can complete more complex tasks; Learning to read	Beginning to understand abstract concepts; Follows more complex instructions and adapts them to suit the situation; Concentration span much increased; Can be absorbed by an activity	Complex questioning develops; Analyses situations and adapts behaviour to it; Increased understanding of abstract concepts; May begin to question what they are told by adults	Increasing pressure to perform well at school; Exploration of subjects may be very intense; Can usually detect when adults are not sure of what they are saying; Questioning examination of everything
Faith	Begins to trust; Realises self is separate from their parents; Senses love of parents and Christian community	Instinctive belief in God; Imitates adult behaviour in church; Expresses wonder, joy, thanksgiving and praise; Begins to use faith language	Asks questions about faith and God; Increasing interest in Bible characters and can identify with them	Identifies with 'my' church; Explores faith; Learning about big issues at school—cloning, genetics, evolution	Challenges Bible stories as the 'truth'; Developing own ideas about interpretation of the Bible	Expands experiences of 'faith'; May have a time of doubt and serious questioning about God's existence; Explores faith issues
Relationship with authority	Likes consistency	Likes consistency	Open to changes but likes to know what is happening	Begins to push accepted boundaries but will usually conform	Pushes boundaries and expects them to be expanding as they get older	Negotiates boundaries with parents and other adults

Personal reflection sheet

What did you learn from this session?

What how will this affect the way you work with children?

How will this affect the way you work with children?

What further items in this area would you like to follow up?

Portfolio checklist

Learning outcomes

❖ To understand how children develop physically, emotionally, intellectually, socially, morally and spiritually.

❖ To appreciate the range of learning styles and approaches that there can be within a group.

❖ To reflect on personal experience of life and faith, and the effects of this on ways of working with children.

❖ To consider work with children in the light of some theories of human development.

To show that the learning outcomes have been achieved, your portfolio must include at least the following. *(Tick when you have included each one in the file.)*

☐ Personal reflection sheet

☐ Any notes taken during CORE Session 1, with any additional ideas

☐ 'Images of faith' sheet and your reflections on it

☐ Any other responses/reflections you wish to include

The participant's involvement in a group for CORE Session 1, 'Child development', is confirmed. The learning outcomes have been achieved through the evidence provided.

Signed (assessor)_____ Date _____

Any comments from assessor

Signed (candidate)_____ Date _____

Reproduced with permission from *Core Skills for Children's Work* (Barnabas for Children, 2013) **www.barnabasinchurches.org.uk**

32 CORE SKILLS

CORE SESSION TWO
Working as a team

Aim

To enable participants to identify and reflect on their current skills and encourage them to actively seek support for themselves in their work with children.

Learning outcomes

✤ To evaluate current skills, gifts, strengths and weaknesses and identify possibilities for personal development.
✤ To recognise the need to feel valued, equipped and supported in their role.
✤ To develop the skills and habit of reflecting on their work with children.

Materials needed

Starters

✤ A selection of everyday objects
✤ Photographs of world leaders
✤ A flipchart, plus newspaper and sticky tape (for 'Teamwork: Tower'), or construction materials and pre-prepared model (for 'Teamwork: Model maker')

Core

✤ Large sheets of paper and pens
✤ Pre-printed slips of paper (for Exercise C)
✤ Elmer story by David McKee (optional)

Worship

✤ Pens and plain postcards or small pieces of paper
✤ CD and CD player

Opening thought

There are different kinds of spiritual gifts, but they all come from the same Spirit. There are different ways to serve the same Lord, and we can each do different things. Yet the same God works in all of us and helps us in everything we do. The Spirit has given each of us a special way of serving others.
1 Corinthians 12:4–7

Starters

Everyday objects

> **You will need:**
> * A selection of everyday objects

Look at a selection of everyday objects: for example, a packet of seeds, a map, a tin of beans and so on. Use these objects to make comments about leadership: for example, 'Being a leader is like/is not like (a packet of seeds, a map, a tin of beans and so on), because…'

Leaders

> **You will need:**
> * Photographs of world leaders

If a set of photographs of current and past world leaders is available, look at them and discuss what are or were the leaders' strengths and weaknesses. Discuss what kind of leader is attractive and why.

Alternatively, share past memories of leaders. 'I admired one leader I remember because…' 'I disliked one leader I remember because…' Attempt to work out what was important to those leaders.

Teamwork

> **You will need:**
> * A flipchart
> * Newspaper and sticky tape (for 'Tower')
> * Construction materials and pre-prepared model (for 'Model maker')

Do one of the following activities.

Tower

> **You will need:**
> * Newspaper and 1m sticky tape per group

In groups of four, use the newspaper and sticky tape to build the tallest tower possible in the time given.

Human knot

In groups of four or five, form a circle, shoulder-to-shoulder. Stretch your arms out in front towards the middle of the circle and join hands with two different people. Wait, holding hands, until everyone is joined. The task for each group now is to untangle and form a new circle without anyone letting go of the hands they are holding. Participants may change their grip so as to be more comfortable, but they are not to unclasp and reclasp so as to undo the knot.

Welded ankle

Mark off beginning and finish lines for a space across which the group must travel. The group assembles behind the start, with their feet touching a neighbour's foot on each side to form an unbroken line. They must travel across the space and over the finish while maintaining continuous contact with their neighbours' feet. If anyone in the group loses contact, the entire group must return to the start.

Model maker

> **You will need:**
> * Bags of construction materials
> * One prepared model

The leader prepares a fairly simple (but not too simple!) model using Lego, K'nex or similar, probably using 20–25 pieces. The participants are given one minute to look at the model before it is taken out of sight.

Each group is given a bag of the exact pieces needed to make an identical model, and must, working together, build an exact replica of the original model (even down to which coloured bricks go where).

A time limit may be set within which the task must be completed to help focus the group (and, incidentally, adding a sense of urgency).

Teamwork debrief and conclusion

Whichever teamwork activity you chose to do, hold a debriefing session, asking the following questions.

* Who took the lead?
* What other roles were identifiable?
* Was everyone made to feel part of the activity?
* How was the contribution of each person valued?
* What words or actions assisted the group?

An alternative means of debriefing is a group sculpture. Once the activity is finished, a volunteer arranges the group in a way that visually represents how the people related or worked together. This might be an abstract form or a re-creation of a still scene from the activity. Allow each person in the group in turn to step out of the sculpture and view it from different angles. The tutor could step in to take the place of each participant in turn as they step out. Allow the participants to comment on the sculpture and suggest how they might change it from their viewpoint, or perhaps how it might change if the group could improve on their performance.

Finally, on a sheet of flipchart paper, draw two columns, one headed 'positive' and one headed 'negative'. List the positive aspects of working as a member of a team, and then the negative aspects.

CORE

What's in a team?

> You will need:
> ✳ Large sheets of paper and pens
> ✳ Pre-printed slips of paper (for Exercise C)

Select from exercise A, B or C. If you are doing this session with a group of colleagues who work together, relate the questions to your specific situation, but otherwise treat them more generally.

Exercise A

Have a group wordstorm on 'Ten things you could do to build a team' (being realistic about time commitments and rotas).

Exercise B

Discuss the following statements. If a team is to be effective:

✤ Team members must be clear about the aim of the group.
✤ Team members must have clear roles.
✤ There must be effective leadership.
✤ Team members must feel that their input is valued.
✤ Team members should trust each other.

Can you recognise ways in which these things do or could happen in a team situation? What could be added?

Exercise C

What needs to happen in a team? Arrange the following phrases according to their importance in a children's ministry team. Add two or three if you think something is missing.

Agree the most important one, then the next most important two, then the next most important three, and so on, to create a pyramid of important elements. Discard one or two if you can all agree.

It will be easier if you have each element printed

on a separate piece of paper so that you can lay them out in priority order on the floor (see page 39 for a photocopiable list).

✤ Develop shared aims
✤ Ensure everyone has a clear role
✤ Have an overall leader
✤ Have someone to represent the team at church meetings
✤ Make everyone feel valued
✤ Arrange social events
✤ Celebrate successes
✤ Give each other feedback
✤ Appreciate each other
✤ Arrange regular planning meetings
✤ Work in pairs
✤ Pray together
✤ Attend training regularly
✤ Develop skills
✤ Bring new workers to join the team
✤ Have a Christmas party
✤ Set a realistic budget
✤ Get support from the whole church
✤ [Add your own suggestions]

Support web

> You will need:
> ✳ Elmer story by David McKee (optional)

Individuals and teams need support. In a football match, there are only eleven players on the pitch for each team at any one time, but there is a huge support network that goes into trying to ensure that the team is as effective as possible: manager, trainer, physiotherapist, scout, doctor, stewards, substitutes, fans and so on. On an aeroplane flight, you only see the pilot and the cabin crew, but there are dozens of people who designed and built the aircraft, keep it maintained, prepare meals, put the steps or ramp in place for you to get on and off, run air traffic control and so on.

Think together about the support you are given as a team of children's workers and as individuals— and, more importantly, what sort of support it is. For example, the church's support may be financial support in the form of a resources budget. The support of partners or family may be in taking on additional tasks or giving permission in some way.

Individually, create a support web on a sheet of paper. This is not to be shared with anyone, but will be used later in worship.

These supporters are as much a part of the team as those who actually do the work, yet sometimes their involvement is not recognised.

You may like to read one of the *Elmer* stories by David McKee (published by Red Fox). The first story, 'Elmer', is suitable. Invite the group to respond to the story.

Who's in a team?

Dr Meredith Belbin, a management consultant, has done some important research into team roles and effective leadership. His work with a large number of managers suggests that there are nine possible team roles that a person can adopt. Some are natural roles, some are roles that a person can adopt if necessary, and some are roles that a person finds very hard to adopt.

Study the roles in the grid on page 40. Which do you think you represent? Which roles might have been displayed in the earlier part of the session? Which roles are missing in the team in which you work?

Job advert

Write a job advert for the team of people you need for the children's work at your church.

Reflection in action

Look at the 'reflection' circle below. Think together about travelling to this session. Did it involve a car? Public transport? Walking? Sharing a lift? Were there any hold-ups? Anything unexpected? How was the timing—too early or on time? Might you do the preparation or the journey differently next time? Use a different route? Leave earlier?

We reflect on so many things during our 'normal' day that it is second nature: we make decisions about the future based upon our reflections on past experiences. But we often don't use this same method in thinking about our work with children. Think back to the last session in which you were involved with children. You have already done the 'Plan' and the 'Do': you now need to 'Reflect' and, as a result of your reflection, decide what you would do differently next time.

Individually, write down each thing you 'Did' in that session, 'Reflect' on it and note your reflections, even if the decision is to do the same next time. Share together any thoughts that come out of doing this exercise.

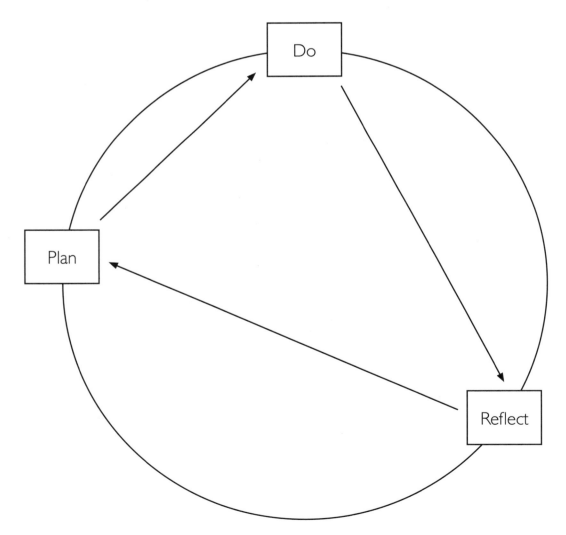

Biblical thought

At times, we can all feel inadequate for the task ahead, but God knows each of us and calls us to work in children's ministry.

Read Psalm 139:1–6 and write down the things about you that God can use in children's ministry, both the obviously good skills, talents and experiences and the less obvious things that God is transforming and using. Share your thoughts with the group if you wish.

Then read Isaiah 42:1–4. Isaiah's prophecy highlights some qualities of the Lord's Servant, which may be important for your ministry.

❖ What helps you to know you are chosen and loved by God?
❖ What helps you to present God's love well without 'shouting or raising your voice'?
❖ Is bringing justice for children part of your ministry?

Read any of the following passages and reflect on what they show of Jesus' leadership styles.

❖ John 2:12–22
❖ John 13:3–6
❖ Luke 2:41–52
❖ Luke 9:1–6
❖ Luke 24:13–35
❖ Mark 6:45–46

When might we choose certain leadership styles, and why?

What makes a good leader? Here are four key qualities:

❖ Leaders have vision.
❖ Leaders attract followers.
❖ Leaders can communicate their vision.
❖ Leaders enable the group to achieve a common goal.

This fourth quality requires many skills and attributes. Make a list together of some that Jesus seemed to possess, and share with each other some Gospel passages that show some of Jesus' skills of leadership and teamwork.

You might like to choose from many other passages that show how Jesus exercised a variety of leadership qualities, and discuss what we can learn from these passages for our own practice. In what situations could certain styles be more effective?

Reflection on learning

What do you bring to the team in which you work? Are there new skills you could develop to enrich the team and complement the other members?

How can you help all the members of the team to play an active role within it?

Are there members of your church who would be willing to be part of the support network for the children's work? How can you encourage them to be involved?

Worship

> You will need:
> ✳ Pens and plain A6 cards
> ✳ CD and CD player

Picture the people who give you support, using the 'support web' drawn earlier (see pages 35–36). Recall the tower building or other team activity, and picture the people who are in your children's work team.

A prayer

For these people, their support, their skills, their friendship and their faith, we give you thanks, Lord.

Suggested song

Brother, sister, let me serve you (*Sing Glory*, Kevin Mayhew)

Group affirmation exercise

Sit in a circle and all take a card. Write your name on one side of the card and place it, face down, in the centre of the circle. Now pick up someone else's card and write a positive appreciation on the reverse. Repeat with other cards if appropriate. Write, 'We thank God for… in the group…', filling in the blank space with a positive comment about the person named.

Finally, working round the group, each read out the affirmation written on the card (but not the name). This will affirm the group for the skills that are contained within it, even though people will not know which comments relate to whom.

Music

Together we are strong (Track 1, *Small World, Big Band Volume 2—More Friends*, Jools Holland and friends) or other appropriate music.

Reading

Read this extract from a book by Albert Schweitzer.

He comes to us as one unknown, without a name, as of old, by the lake-side, he came to those men who knew him not. He speaks to us the same word: 'Follow thou me!' and sets us the task, which he has to fulfil for our time. He commands. And to those who obey him, whether they be wise or simple, he will reveal himself in the toils, the conflicts, the sufferings which they shall pass through in his fellowship, and as an ineffable mystery, they shall learn in their own experience who he is.

Albert Schweitzer, *The Spiritual Life* (Ecco Press, 1996)

Sending out

Invite the participants to take their cards home and perhaps add a passport-sized photograph later.

> What we are is God's gift to us.
>
> Who we become is our gift to God.
>
> Eleanor Powell

What's in a team? Exercise C

Photocopy and cut out these phrases if you wish to arrange them in priority order on the floor.

- ❖ Develop shared aims
- ❖ Ensure everyone has a clear role
- ❖ Have an overall leader
- ❖ Have someone to represent the team at church meetings
- ❖ Make everyone feel valued
- ❖ Arrange social events
- ❖ Celebrate successes
- ❖ Give each other feedback
- ❖ Appreciate each other
- ❖ Arrange regular planning meetings
- ❖ Work in pairs
- ❖ Pray together
- ❖ Attend training regularly
- ❖ Develop skills
- ❖ Bring new workers to join the team
- ❖ Have a Christmas party
- ❖ Set a realistic budget
- ❖ Get support from the whole church
- ❖ [Add your own suggestions]

Reproduced with permission from *Core Skills for Children's Work* (Barnabas for Children, 2013) www.barnabasinchurches.org.uk

Who's in a team? Belbin's team roles

❖ **Plant:** very creative, the ideas person. The person who often has a game or activity to suggest for each week's theme.

❖ **Resource Investigator:** extravert, good at making outside contacts and developing ideas. A leader able to bring new people into the children's groups, involve helpers and suggest someone or something to add to what is planned.

❖ **Monitor Evaluator:** shrewd and prudent, analytical. A children's worker who takes a broader look at what the children's group is achieving, making suggestions for the medium term, having ideas for longer-term development.

❖ **Shaper:** dynamic and challenging. The children's worker with new ideas and different ways of doing things, seeing chances to change the church's patterns.

❖ **Coordinator:** respected, mature and good at ensuring that talents are used effectively. A good leader of the children's ministry, drawing people in and playing to their strengths.

❖ **Implementer:** practical, loyal and task-orientated. The group leader who can always be relied on to be there and be dependable in seeing to the practical necessities for the children and the leaders.

❖ **Completer Finisher:** meticulous and with attention to detail, also full of nervous energy. The children's worker who makes sure everything has been thought of and is well organised.

❖ **Team Worker:** caring and very people-orientated. The person on the children's team who looks out for everyone on the team, checking that they are happy and supported.

❖ **Specialist:** high technical skill, and professional as opposed to organisational prime loyalties. Could be the artistic one or the person who can get children involved with the computer or the music—they love that special interest.

Reproduced with permission from *Core Skills for Children's Work* (Barnabas for Children, 2013) www.barnabasinchurches.org.uk

Personal reflection sheet

What did you learn from this session?

How will this affect the way you work with children?

What further items in this area would you like to follow up?

Reproduced with permission from *Core Skills for Children's Work* (Barnabas for Children, 2013) www.barnabasinchurches.org.uk

CORE SESSION 2: WORKING AS A TEAM 41

Portfolio checklist

Learning outcomes

❖ To evaluate current skills, gifts, strengths and weaknesses, and identify possibilities for personal development.
❖ To recognise the need to feel valued, equipped and supported in their role.
❖ To develop the skills and habit of reflecting on their work with children.

To show that the learning outcomes have been achieved, your portfolio must include at least the following. *(Tick when you have included each one in the file.)*

☐ Personal reflection sheet

☐ Notes taken during Session 2, with any additional ideas

☐ Your comments and ideas about being part of a team

☐ Your reflection exercise on a session with children

☐ Your support web and any affirming items from worship

☐ Any other responses/reflections you wish to include

The participant's involvement in a group for CORE Session 2, 'Working as a team', is confirmed. The learning outcomes have been achieved through the evidence provided.

Signed (assessor)_____ Date _____

Any comments from assessor

Signed (candidate)_____ Date _____

CORE SESSION THREE
Programme planning

Aim

To develop an understanding of how children learn and the skills required to deliver a programme relevant to their needs.

Learning outcomes

❖ To understand how learning styles in childhood differ, and are influenced by society and culture.
❖ To work creatively with children, using a variety of learning styles.
❖ To plan original sessions and deliver published programmes to meet the needs of children.
❖ To develop the practice of reflecting on and evaluating sessions.

Materials needed

Starters

❖ An apple
❖ French objects

Core

❖ Flipchart
❖ *Alfie Gives a Hand* by Shirley Hughes (published by Red Fox) or similar story
❖ A selection of published material for children: for example, Roots, Scripture Union material, pages from a website, and so on
❖ Copies of the 'Selecting published material' chart on page 48
❖ Resources for children's groups that have been found useful
❖ A range of current worship and learning materials
❖ Paper and pens
❖ Post-it notes

Worship

❖ Headphones
❖ A book
❖ A picture
❖ A pair of shoes
❖ Labels: aural, reading/writing, visual, kinaesthetic
❖ Post-it notes

Opening thought

They said to Jesus, 'We need more confidence!' Jesus said, 'A bit of trust is all you need, the sort a gardener has. If you have a small seed you can make it grow into a large plant. Or you can transplant a bush from a garden to a new position by the sea and it will thrive.'
Luke 17:5–6 (from John Henson, *Good as New*, O Books, 2004)

Starters

Apple

> **You will need:**
> * An apple

Set an apple in the centre of the group. How could it be used? Call out as many uses as possible in two minutes. Ask each person, if they had to choose only one use, what would it be and why? Then ask each person to think of a child they know. What might that child choose?

France

This activity can be based on a different country of the world, if that would be easier to prepare.

> **You will need:**
> * French objects

Pass round:

* A baguette and a round of Camembert. Invite everyone to break off bits to eat as the other items are passed round.
* A euro.
* A souvenir from France.
* A travel brochure for France.
* A picture from a French gallery.
* A guidebook held open with elastic bands at a page of text with a picture of a French city.
* A library book on the history of France, open at a page of text.

When all the items have been circulated, tell of an experience in France.

CORE

Learning styles

> **You will need:**
> * Flipchart
> * *Alfie Gives a Hand* by Shirley Hughes, or similar story

A number of theories have been developed about the different ways in which people learn, and which styles an individual might find most helpful. There is no 'best style' that fits everyone or that everyone needs to use; they all have advantages.

It is useful if those preparing sessions are aware of their own learning preference, because there can be a tendency to use the preferred style most often. Deliberately varying the learning style being used in a group enriches the experience for everyone.

What can you recall from the exercise about France? Do members of the group differ in what they remember first? Why?

The following are some labels given to learning styles in a model called VARK.

Which do you think best describes you?

* **Visual:** Learn best by seeing (pictures, diagrams, multimedia and so on). Enjoy finding a new place by using a map.
* **Aural:** Learn best by hearing (a discussion, a speaker who tells stories to illustrate a point and so on). Enjoy debate and exploring ideas out loud.
* **Read/Write:** Learn best by reading (a leaflet, handout, written information and so on). Enjoy looking up information in text.
* **Kinaesthetic:** Learn best through action (trying things out, doing activities alongside someone else, and so on). Enjoy getting out and doing things.

Clearly no one learns in only one style, but most people have a clear preference. A variety of styles can be helpful to individuals and is a must to include everyone in a group.

There are fun questionnaires online to find out more about your learning style. VARK is only one example; typing 'learning styles' into an internet search engine will turn up a multitude of possibilities.

On the flipchart, list different methods that could be used to explore the parable of the lost sheep (Luke 15:1–7) with a group of children that includes all the above learning styles.

Discuss ways in which a children's picture book such as *Alfie Gives a Hand* by Shirley Hughes can be used:

* To make a point about sharing.
* As a stimulus for making a model.
* As the beginning of a discussion about hunting for something lost.
* For remembering experiences together.
* For talking about the way we try something to find out how it works.

Planning a session

NAOMIE

The acronym NAOMIE is a mnemonic to aid preparation.

* **Need:** What do the children need? What do we, the leaders (and any other interested adults), need?
* **Aim:** What should be achieved by the end of the session?
* **Objectives:** What are the smaller goals that work together to achieve the aim?
* **Method:** What methods will be used? What talents are there to be used? Are they varied? Are they suitable for use with different children? Is there a balance of active and reflective methods? Is the programme inclusive?
* **Implementation:** Does everyone know his or her responsibilities? Is everyone able to do what is required of him or her?
* **Evaluation:** How did it go? What went well? Why? Did the session fulfil the aim? What could have been better? How? What needs to be remembered next time? (Anecdotes can contribute to evaluation.)

Selecting published material

> You will need:
> * A selection of published material for children: for example, Roots, Scripture Union material, pages from a website, and so on
> * Copies of the 'Selecting published material' chart on page 48

What matters when choosing which material to use? Using the chart on page 48, rate each statement from 1 to 5, with 1 being 'very important' and 5 'not important at all'.

Examine a selection of materials and see which product(s) most closely fulfil(s) the needs identified.

Using published material

The following pointers could be answered with a quick 'yes/no'. However, you may want to respond 'Maybe, if…'

* Should every leader have his or her own copy of the material?
* Would you write on your copy?
* Should material be selected bearing in mind learning styles—of both leaders and children?
* Should the leaders meet to prepare? How often?
* Might material be prepared which is not used?

Finally, think about what simple ways can be adopted to ensure that everyone knows who is doing or bringing what for a session. How can people let others know if they can't attend?

Being flexible

There may be times when you find that the material you planned to use is not appropriate—for example, after a death or celebration, if your space is unavailable, or the children are very excited, and so on. In these situations you need to be flexible about the session and be prepared to change the plan either on the spot or at short notice. This can be a challenge but being prepared for the unexpected will help you to cope well with the session.

Can you identify situations that might cause you to abandon your planned session? A contingency plan might be helpful.

Practice

> You will need:
> * Resources for children's groups
> * A range of current worship and learning materials

Divide into two groups to plan a session for a specific group of children (real or imagined). Ask one group to use a published programme (either one they are used to, or an unfamiliar one) as the basis for the session. Ask the other group to use material from a variety of sources, selecting from those provided and choosing a theme relevant to their community.

Look at and briefly discuss the NAOMIE method of planning (see above) before starting. Afterwards, share the resulting session plans and discuss how they might work. If possible, use the plans to run a real session, and meet together afterwards to discuss how well they worked. Comment on the work of the other group.

Devise a way of reflecting on a session as soon as it finishes, based on the 'Evaluation' part of NAOMIE.

Evaluating other resources

Spend ten minutes discussing the following questions.

* Where can resources be found?
* What resources have others found useful, and why?
* What works well for leaders and for children?
* How is that evaluation made?
* What are the key things to look for in a resource?

Questions

> You will need:
> * Paper and pens

Asking questions is often used as a method in children's groups, but there are many sorts of questions and different reasons for asking them. Make a list of reasons for asking questions.

Some questions are 'open': for example, 'What might it feel like to be lost?' Some are 'closed': for example, 'How many sheep were lost?' Different types of question are appropriate or inappropriate in different circumstances.

Thinking about the Bible story of Jesus' baptism (Matthew 3:13–17), look at the questions below. Which might be used or not, and why?

* Who was there? What was the name of the river?
* What did John say? What did Jesus say? What did God say?
* What sounds would the people watching hear?
* What might the people be thinking?
* What would you ask if you were there?

Further discussion or reflection on the topic of questions should include:

* What are the pros and cons of beginning a session with the question 'Who can remember what we did last week?'
* What types of question should be avoided?
* What are helpful responses to answers given to questions?

Play

> You will need:
> * Post-it notes
> * Flipchart

Play is a vital way of learning for children. Individually, bring to mind a favourite play activity from your childhood. Draw or briefly describe it on a Post-it note, and stick the note on the flipchart. Now, on that flipchart sheet, add a list of the opportunities for play that exist in the life of your church today.

Discuss the following quotation: 'The main characteristic of play—child or adult—is not its content, but its mode. Play is an approach to action, not a form of activity' (Jerome Bruner, quoted in Janet Moyles, *Just Playing?*, OUP, 1989).

When might play feature in a session—at the beginning, in the middle, or at the end?

What are the advantages of each? Think of some examples.

How can you provide space for play within your teaching session?

Biblical thought

Jesus used different teaching styles, which met the differing preferences of his hearers and disciples. Some examples are:

* The good Samaritan (aural): Luke 10:30–37
* A tree and its fruit (visual): Matthew 12:33
* The feeding of the five thousand (kinaesthetic): Matthew 14:13–21; Mark 6:30–44; Luke 9:10–17; John 6:1–14

There is a lack of reference in the Bible to reading and writing, as most people in Jesus' time did not have these skills. Interestingly, most of our teaching and learning now involves reading. The passage in which Jesus reads the scriptures, in Luke 4:16–22, shows how special and different reading was.

Discuss more examples of the varieties of learning that happened when people were with Jesus. Look at his actions, his ways of talking and the types of questions he used.

Reflection on learning

* What is important to remember when leading a session with children? Why?
* What are some good methods for involving children in evaluation, using pictures, words or conversations?
* How were questions used in this session?
* Listen for questions in a future session; make a list and reflect on their use.

Worship

> You will need:
> * Headphones
> * A book
> * A picture
> * A pair of shoes
> * Labels: aural, reading/writing, visual, kinaesthetic
> * Post-it notes

Lay the objects out with the appropriate label. Encourage participants to write their name on a Post-it note and place it next to the learning style they are least comfortable using. Ask the participants to take a name from a learning style that they are confident using and pray for that person, asking for the gifts they need. Close the time of worship using the following prayer:

Loving Lord, we offer the gifts and talents we have to serve the children in our care. Give us the confidence to vary the activities in our programmes to stimulate them and encourage them to grow in relationship with you. Amen

Selecting published material

Rate the following statements from 1 to 5, with 1 being 'very important' and 5 'not important at all'.

1.	The resource offers a stand-alone selection of material for each week throughout the year.	1	2	3	4	5
2.	It highlights all the festivals of the Christian year.	1	2	3	4	5
3.	It gives plenty of choices for a wide range of ages of children in one resource.	1	2	3	4	5
4.	It uses inclusive language.	1	2	3	4	5
5.	It has plenty of ideas of things to make and do.	1	2	3	4	5
6.	Material written for use with children links with companion material for a whole congregation.	1	2	3	4	5
7.	Suggestions are given for worship when all ages are together.	1	2	3	4	5
8.	It is inexpensive.	1	2	3	4	5
9.	It is brightly coloured.	1	2	3	4	5
10.	It can be picked up and used easily.	1	2	3	4	5
11.	Someone trustworthy recommended it.	1	2	3	4	5
12.	The local church has always used it.	1	2	3	4	5
13.	It is photocopiable.	1	2	3	4	5
14.	It is firmly biblically based.	1	2	3	4	5
15.	It has a spiritual element.	1	2	3	4	5
16.	It follows the Revised Common Lectionary.	1	2	3	4	5
17.	It contains plenty of web links and resources on the website.	1	2	3	4	5
18.	Everything comes in the pack.	1	2	3	4	5
19.	Activity papers are included.	1	2	3	4	5

Reproduced with permission from *Core Skills for Children's Work* (Barnabas for Children, 2013) **www.barnabasinchurches.org.uk**

Personal reflection sheet

What did you learn from this session?

How will this affect the way you work with children?

What further items in this area would you like to follow up?

Reproduced with permission from *Core Skills for Children's Work* (Barnabas for Children, 2013) www.barnabasinchurches.org.uk

Portfolio checklist

Learning outcomes

❖ To understand how learning styles in childhood differ, and are influenced by society and culture.
❖ To work creatively with children, using a variety of learning styles.
❖ To plan original sessions and deliver published programmes to meet the needs of children.
❖ To develop the practice of reflecting on and evaluating sessions.

To show that the learning outcomes have been achieved, your portfolio must include at least the following. *(Tick when you have included each one in the file.)*

☐ Personal reflection sheet

☐ Notes taken during Session 3, with any additional ideas

☐ A description of your learning style

☐ The session you planned with the group

☐ An outline of a session you have used and your evaluation of it, using the method you devised

☐ Any other responses/reflections you wish to include

The participant's involvement in a group for CORE Session 3, 'Programme planning', is confirmed. The learning outcomes have been achieved through the evidence provided.

Signed (assessor)_____ Date _____

Any comments from assessor

Signed (candidate)_____ Date _____

CORE SESSION FOUR
Children and community

Aim

To explore ways of working among children in a variety of contexts beyond the local church.

Learning outcomes

❖ To reflect on stories from different contexts and distil principles of good practice.
❖ To develop strategies for developing new areas of work with children in a variety of contexts.
❖ To explore an understanding of what it means to be 'church'.
❖ To advocate the active participation of children in mission and ministry.

Materials needed

Starters

❖ Flipchart sheets
❖ Pens
❖ Pieces of paper of postcard size
❖ 56 2p coins or counters

Core

❖ Stories photocopied from page 56
❖ Three large sheets of paper
❖ Pens

Worship

❖ Picture or model of a sheepfold
❖ Pieces of A4 card
❖ Pencils
❖ Scissors
❖ Reflective music

Opening thought

Children have a ministry both within and beyond the church community. They may act as evangelists among their friends or families. Many parents have been drawn to Christian commitment through their children. Children may have an apostolic ministry in being sent out to the places where children are, making Christ present in the world. Within the playground, they may work against bullying and racism, befriend the lonely or show a generosity of spirit, all of which makes the Spirit of Christ evident in other children.
CGMC, *Unfinished Business* 5.12

'When you welcome one of these children because of me, you welcome me.'
Matthew 18:5

Starters

Wordstorm

> You will need:
> * Flipchart sheets
> * Pens

In small groups, wordstorm all the good things that happen in the work among children in your church community.

Church or not church?

> You will need:
> * Pieces of paper of postcard size
> * Pens

On separate small pieces of paper, write down the numerous different activities that children might be involved with in their community. The activities should include a wide range of things: some that are clearly 'church' (for example, meeting with friends to pray), some that could be church outreach (for example, playing football), and some things that are definitely not church (for example, horse riding, life saving, judo and so on).

When the task is complete, sort the activities into piles of 'church' and 'not church' according to whether the activities could be a form of church. Discuss why they belong in one pile or another. Is it the activities or the context in which they are done that makes them 'church'? What is the difference between 'church' and the local Christian community?

Where are the children?

> You will need:
> * 56 2p coins or counters

Challenge the group to put the coins into separate piles to create visual representations of the following statistics concerning children and your community. Use the piles of coins as a way to reflect together on your own church's mission with and among children.

Not in church

If all the children in your community are represented by 20 coins, how many will be part of a church and how many will be found elsewhere?
Answer: One in church and 19 elsewhere.

Not with you on Sunday/your meeting day

If the seven days of the week are represented by 21 coins, how many will be a Sunday or the day your children's group meets?
Answer: Three are Sunday/your meeting day and 18 are the rest of the week.

So where are the children?

If we assume that children sleep for 56 hours of the 168 hours in a week, that leaves 112 waking hours. Using all 56 coins/counters, how does the group think this time is divided up?
Answer: 56 coins: 1 at a church event; 17 in school; 38 hours at home, travelling or playing with friends.

What are the implications of these figures for your church's work with children in the community?

Aims for reaching new children

Look through the following list of possible aims. Which *three* of these would you choose as the aims of your group? Which would be your main aim? Are there any of these aims that your church needs to discard deliberately?

* To get more people to church on Sundays.
* To serve the local community by blessing children and parents with a variety of resources and events.
* For children to have fun.
* To teach children about God, Jesus and the Bible, giving them a vocabulary of faith that can play a part in our dialogue with them as they grow up.
* To show that the church cares about children.
* To remind a generation of the concept of right and wrong.
* To call children to become disciples and follow Jesus wholeheartedly.
* To give children a chance to worship.
* To make the leaders feel needed.
* To provide a child-minding service for hard-working parents.
* To bring families to faith.
* To bring children to faith.
* To make our church look good.
* To let each child know that God loves them personally.
* To connect people on the edge of church with the congregation that meets on Sunday.
* To help children own the church building.
* To 'plant acorns that will one day turn into oak trees'.
* Other (add your own suggestions)…

CORE

Working among children in different contexts

> You will need:
> ✳ Stories photocopied from page 56

For 200 years, many, if not most, children in Britain and Ireland received Christian teaching and nurture in Sunday school. Today, the whole ethos of Sunday has changed. Many people regard Sunday as a day for various shopping, DIY or leisure activities, or for spending time with separated parents or grandparents. A large majority of families in today's society have no contact with the church whatsoever.

The settings in which churches work with children are now more varied than ever. Rural, urban and suburban communities often have very different needs, and the multicultural and multifaith facets of society bring rich possibilities. Changes in the view of the place of the child in society have been mirrored by changes in the church's attitude towards children.

Much has been written about different ways and styles that make it possible, in this new situation, for children and families to be in contact and involved with activities of the church community.

For all these reasons, large numbers of children participate in church activities midweek, and informal teaching is offered in a wide variety of contexts and situations. Although these events may not happen in a church building, these children are perceived as being part of the church community or simply 'being church', whether they have contact with the church on Sunday or not. Such new expressions give many children and young families, who would otherwise be denied it, access to the Christian message and to safe and loving Christian communities. Many church members now see activities other than Sunday worship as 'church', and groups other than the Sunday congregation as 'church'.

In small groups, look at two or three of the stories copied from page 56.

In the light of these stories, discuss:

❖ What makes these activities successful?
❖ What are the principles underlying them? (For example, relationships, being on the children's 'turf', fun, creativity, space just to 'be'.)
❖ What principles could you take from these clubs and apply to your own situation?
❖ What things are not applicable to your situation, and why not?

❖ How are these activities an expression of 'church'?
❖ What is already happening or could happen where you are, which is a new expression of being church?

A strategy for new work in church communities

In small groups, work through the following five steps, allowing equal time for each one. Group with others from the same church or in mixed groups, where each participant thinks about their own community and church but shares their thinking with the group as they go along.

There will be insufficient time in the session to do more than begin each step and raise some of the issues. It is hoped that participants will wish to continue or take discussions further individually, together or in their church group.

Step 1: Identify the needs of an area

> You will need:
> ✳ Two large sheets of paper
> ✳ Pens

In the centre of a large sheet of paper, draw a symbol to represent children. Around the symbol, write down the needs of the children in the community. Their needs might be physical, spiritual, emotional, mental or social.

In the centre of a second sheet, draw the same symbol and write the name of your area underneath. Write down all the different things (people, organisations and activities) in the area that relate to the children. (They may include schools, parent and toddler groups, community workers, health visitors, and leisure activities.)

If you don't know all that is available, how could you find it out?

On the second sheet, underneath the people, organisations and activities, write down what needs these things aim to meet. Think about and list the needs that remain unmet.

After this session, talk with a group of children from your church, school or community group to find out their needs and interests (taking care not to raise expectations that cannot be met).

Step 2: Acknowledge the skills of the church community

> You will need:
> ✳ A large sheet of paper
> ✳ Pens

Draw a picture of a church building in the centre of a large sheet of paper. Wordstorm all the different assets the church has, both physical (the building, facilities, equipment and so on) and availability of people and skills (include life skills and personality types: for example, the grandmother figure who gets alongside children, making them feel special, and the 'spiritual' person who is able to offer prayerful support).

Step 3: Identify strengths and weaknesses of the church community

What is your church able to offer to the local community? Are there ways in which your church can meet the needs of the local area? A good way of making this assessment is to look at your church using the SWOT analysis system.

* **Strengths:** what is being done and the resources, people and buildings available.
* **Weaknesses:** what you fail to do, or do ineffectively.
* **Opportunities** in the local community. For example, the needs and opportunities that are there to reach out to children, or the opportunities to share with the congregation of your church.
* **Threats:** the potential stumbling blocks. For example, the limits of the church building, the limited number of people to do the work, people with insufficient skills and knowledge, and so on.

The church needs to be aware of current initiatives and local and national government legislation. Current laws and regulations affect the way we do things. These factors might be considered in the SWOT analysis.

Step 4: Plan aims and strategy

Select one or two needs of the local area, which you think need consideration. How might you start to meet these needs? How will you know when you have met them? One planning method is the use of SMART goals. Here is the CORE version.

* **Specific:** For example, an aim that says, 'to be there for local children' is good but too vague. You will never know if you've met it, and then people will get discouraged. An aim 'to provide regular opportunities for local children to talk about what is troubling them' is a lot clearer.
* **Measurable:** For example, 'by the end of August we will have run a holiday club for one week'.
* **Attributable:** Tasks should be assigned to specific people so that everyone is aware of their responsibilities.

* **Realistic:** The task should be a small step forward, not a giant leap. The aim should be attainable: for example, 'the weekly after-school club should have at least five new members by Christmas' rather than 'the after-school club should triple its membership by next month'.
* **Timebound:** The goal should be attained within a specific timescale, giving you a clear indicator of achievement. Having a timebound goal enables you to look back and, if you've set your goals right, celebrate your success.

Step 5: Achieve the goal

Once your goal is set, a plan needs to be drawn up and broken down into tasks that need to be achieved to meet that goal. You will need to set a timeframe and decide who is responsible for each task. In addition, there should be someone checking that the whole task is on target.

Biblical thought

In small groups, read one of the following Bible passages: Isaiah 58; Matthew 18:1–6; Matthew 25:31–46; Matthew 28:18–20.

* Why should we be concerned about children in different contexts?
* What might each passage have to say on this issue?

Reflection on learning

* What concerns and challenges has this session raised for you?
* What potential benefits do you see for the children in your group and for your church community?
* What would you like to explore further?
* What action will you take or encourage your church community to take as a result of this session?

Worship

> You will need:
> * Picture or model of a sheepfold
> * Pieces of A4 card
> * Pencils
> * Scissors
> * Reflective music

In the centre of the room, create a sheepfold as a focus. Read John 10:7–9, about the door and the sheepfold. Draw round your foot on a piece of card and cut out the shape.

Think about the sheepfold as one that the children can move in and out of, to find a safe, supportive and receptive church community. Think about the steps that could be taken to ensure that this happens in your community. These thoughts can be written on the foot shape during a time of silence or appropriate peaceful music. Place the feet in front of the sheepfold.

In a time of prayer, thank God for the strengths of the church in which you worship and for opportunities to be 'church' in your local community. Pray for God's help in overcoming obstacles in what you plan to do.

A prayer

Loving Lord, open our eyes to see the need for change within our communities, give us the vision to take up these opportunities, and grant us the humility to accept those things we cannot change. Amen

Suitable hymns and songs

The Spirit lives to set us free (*Mission Praise*, Marshall Pickering)

Loving shepherd of thy sheep (*Hymns for Today's Church*, Hodder & Stoughton)

As we are gathered (*Songs of Fellowship*, Kingsway)

He came down that we may have love (*Many and Great*, Wild Goose Publications)

Church and children in different contexts

Travelling church

An urban church has converted a bus, which travels around local estates, offering monthly after-school activities and worship for children aged 7–11. The church is meeting people where they are, and children and their families are hearing about God in a relevant way. The church anticipates that, in time, sustainable Christian communities will develop in these areas.

Summer club

About 50 children of primary school age live on an estate near the church in a suburban village. The church runs a summer club, with 15 children aged 8–13 attending. Initially, every family on the estate was visited and leaflets were delivered. The club meets twice weekly throughout the summer holidays in a variety of venues, and involves a wide range of activities (fishing, farm visits, games and so on). There is no formal Christian teaching except when discussions arise spontaneously.

The local school

A small group from a church decided to pray for their local primary school. Church members built positive relationships with the school by offering to hear children read, volunteering to help at events, being governors and being on the parent–teacher association. They have been invited to lead a weekly assembly, sharing Bible stories with the children. Their prayer is that this will develop into opportunities to contribute to RE lessons, lead an after-school Christian club and invite the school to use their church for a curriculum visit around Christmas and Easter.

Messy Church

Aware that they were not reaching many new families with children at their monthly family service, a church on a housing estate on the edge of a big city decided to re-imagine church for all ages. They chose to hold their Messy Church on a Thursday after school. It begins with a welcome and relaxed hospitality before an hour of exploring a Bible theme with a variety of crafts and activities. Then everyone gathers for a short celebration, including a Bible story, a song and simple interactive prayers. Finally there is a hot meal for everyone. Messy Church welcomes many who have never come to church before.

Festival activities

A church provided a Saturday club in the run-up to Christmas, telling the Christmas story and making decorations and presents. It culminated in a candlelit service for the children and their parents and the whole church family on Christmas Eve. This venture was so successful that it will be extended to a club during Lent.

Church football team

A church was losing all the boys from its children's group to football, cricket and so on. It changed the timing of the group and recruited a football team, which included former members of the group, to take part in a local league.

Dads and toddlers

A suburban church noticed that many dads were looking after their very young children on a Saturday morning. The church offered its hall as a hospitable place for them to meet, providing bacon sandwiches, newspapers, friendship and toys for the children. A number of the dads have found it possible in this context to chat about life and faith. Some have explored Christianity on a short course. For the dads and their children, this has become their weekly church.

Ecumenical midweek club

Churches in several villages in the Scottish Borders had no children's work, although there were many children living in the community. They pooled their resources to provide an ecumenical midweek after-school club. On a quarterly basis, this links into the family service, which is hosted by each church in turn.

Reproduced with permission from *Core Skills for Children's Work* (Barnabas for Children, 2013) www.barnabasinchurches.org.uk

Personal reflection sheet

What did you learn from this session?

How will this affect the way you work with children?

What further items in this area would you like to follow up?

Reproduced with permission from *Core Skills for Children's Work* (Barnabas for Children, 2013) www.barnabasinchurches.org.uk

CORE SESSION 4: CHILDREN AND COMMUNITY **57**

Portfolio checklist

Learning outcomes

❖ To reflect on stories from different contexts and distil principles of good practice.
❖ To develop strategies for developing new areas of work with children in a variety of contexts.
❖ To explore an understanding of what it means to be church.
❖ To advocate the active participation of children in mission and ministry.

To show that the learning outcomes have been achieved, your portfolio must include at least the following. *(Tick when you have included each one in the file.)*

☐ Personal reflection sheet

☐ Any notes you have taken during Session 4

☐ Your ideas in response to 'Aims for reaching new children' (page 52)

☐ Lists of the needs of your area

☐ SWOT analysis of your church

☐ Any other answers/reflections you wish to include

The participant's involvement in a group for CORE Session 4, 'Children and community', is confirmed. The learning outcomes have been achieved through the evidence provided.

Signed (assessor)_____ Date _____

```
Any comments from assessor




```

Signed (candidate)_____ Date _____

Reproduced with permission from *Core Skills for Children's Work* (Barnabas for Children, 2013) www.barnabasinchurches.org.uk

58 CORE SKILLS

CORE SESSION FIVE
Pastoral awareness

Aim

To explore the pastoral issues involved in working with children and reflect on practice.

Learning outcomes

❖ To share insights about a variety of pastoral issues.
❖ To explore how power is used in working with children.
❖ To identify issues involved in providing a safe environment, physically, emotionally and spiritually, for children.

Materials needed

Starters

❖ An appropriate theme tune

Core

❖ Flipchart
❖ Sheets of paper and pens
❖ Photographs of children (cut from newspapers and magazines) showing different ages/races/abilities, different contexts, different emotions and/or postcards collected from art galleries, commercial sets from publishers and greetings cards

Opening thought

'It will be terrible for people who cause even one of my little followers to sin. Those people would be better off thrown into the ocean with a heavy stone tied around their necks.'
Mark 9:42

Starters

Who will it be?

> You will need:
> * Appropriate theme tune (see below)

Read out the following story of how not to start a training session, complete with CD player and appropriate theme tune if it is available.

This is the story of a training session carried out one evening, far away from here. The group of leaders sat close together on hard, uncomfortable chairs, in a cold room with a stale smell. In came the trainer, tall and intimidating—like an old teacher who had walked so many times into so many classrooms full of so many pupils. He placed a tape recorder on the floor and switched it on. As the tape started, he announced that he would shortly be picking someone to act out the character from the tape. Across the room came the well-known tune of a children's television programme.

The participants in the group didn't know where to look. Some looked at the floor, some stared at the ceiling and some looked the trainer straight in the eye in order to take him on. As the music drew to an end, the group became more nervous: they had not come to the training session to be humiliated, but to learn. The trainer then walked round the group, ready to pounce on his victim. He picked the quietest leader, who by now was in a cold sweat…

Discuss the story together, including questions such as:

* What might the leaders have felt when the trainer came in?
* How might they have reacted to the task?
* What might have happened next?

Leaders in children's groups have the power to encourage and affirm, but also to embarrass and humiliate. It is quite possible, with every good intention, to undertake activities with children, assuming that they will like them, without taking time to find out what the group's reactions are. That way, we can end up making some members of the group feel discontented or uncomfortable.

Behind the door

Individually, think quietly about a time when you entered an unfamiliar situation—perhaps a time when you had to go through a door, not knowing who or what was behind it. Can you remember how you felt? What made you feel uncomfortable or comfortable? What did you find behind the door?

In small groups, share this experience of going into the unknown. As a whole group, talk about a scene such as the one in the film *Billy Elliot* where Billy enters the ballet class or audition room. Discuss what his feelings might have been.

What might it feel like for young people to join a minority activity, such as ballet for boys?

What might it feel like for a child to cross the threshold of the church for the first time? What are the negative or positive things about the experience?

CORE

Power

> You will need:
> * Flipchart
> * Sheets of paper and pens

In small groups, discuss the following questions. Record your answers on flipchart paper.

* Who has the most power in the running of your children's group?
* Give some examples of how leaders can use power to have a positive impact on a children's group.
* Give some examples of how leaders can use power to have a negative impact on a children's group.
* Read Luke 2:41–50. Who had the power in this situation? Why do you think Jesus' parents failed to see the purpose of Jesus' activity? Give examples of how we fail to allow children to express their opinions and how we devalue their role in the church.

All together, share points from the discussions.

Charter for Children and the Church

Read the Charter for Children and the Church from the United Reformed Church (below). Does this resemble the church you know?

1. Children are equal partners with adults in the life of the church.
2. The full diet of Christian worship is for children as well as adults.

3. Learning is for the whole church—adults and children.

4. Fellowship is for all, each belonging meaningfully to the rest.

5. Service is for children to give, as well as adults.

6. The call to evangelism comes to all God's people of whatever age.

7. The Holy Spirit speaks powerfully through children as well as adults.

8. The discovery and development of gifts in children and adults is a key function of the church.

9. As a church community, we must learn to do only those things in separate age groups which we cannot in all conscience do together.

10. The concept of the 'priesthood of all believers' includes children.

Misusing power in worship

In small groups, share positive experiences of involving children in the life of the church. Then read over the list on page 65 and discuss how children can be damaged, marginalised, neglected, ignored, excluded, demeaned or emotionally misused.

Behaviour

Every single one of us, child and adult alike, is precious to God, made in God's image and for God's glory, made to become like Christ and be fashioned by his Spirit. Every single one of us is also vulnerable at different times and in different ways, whatever our age, experience and devotion to the Lord and to our ministry. We can all be vulnerable to temptation, tiredness, irritability, loss of self-control and unguarded words and actions.

The value that Jesus places on a child is immense, and he wants us to value children in the same way: we ignore this fact at our peril! It is not that he wants fear to be the motivation for our response to children, but he does want our hearts to beat to the same rhythm as his when it comes to loving and respecting them.

The principles embraced by churches in their child protection policies are designed to support and protect each adult and young person in the complex strengths and vulnerabilities of our relationships with each other. The principles are not intended to threaten work with children but to support it and to strengthen the sense of personal and team responsibility.

In small groups or all together, answer the following questions:

❖ What words or forms of speech would you not use in front of a child, and why?

❖ In what ways do we 'control' children in our children's group? For example, can we run a children's group without shouting?

A Core session exploring issues around challenging behaviour and identifying mechanisms for dealing with it can be found in *More Core Skills* (Barnabas for Children, 2010).

The basics for a positive session with children

Look at the list of requirements for a positive session, on page 66. Discuss your responses, sharing situations when you have met the children's needs in any of these ways, and adding any others to the list.

Pastoral issues: Listening to children

Listening is an important skill that needs constant practice. Listening is not waiting for your turn to speak; it is an activity in its own right.

You could try this game.

> **You will need:**
> * Instruction cards 1, 2 and 3
> * Flipchart paper and pens

Divide the group into pairs: person A and person B. Give an instruction card (1, 2 or 3) to all As. A should not tell B what is written on their card. Ask all Bs to start talking to their partner for two or three minutes about what they have done during the previous week. While they are talking, A follows the instructions on their card.

❖ **Instruction card 1:** Interrupt your partner continually by telling them what *you* have done this week.

❖ **Instruction card 2:** Don't say anything in response to what your partner tells you and, by your body language and facial expressions, show that you are bored.

❖ **Instruction card 3:** Ask your partner some questions but ensure that you do not listen to the answers.

Gather the whole group together. Ask the pairs who had instruction card 1 to share what it felt like during their conversation; repeat the sharing for those with instruction cards 2 and 3. Having reflected on their feelings, ask the group what skills are needed to be a good listener, and write them on to the flipchart paper. Here are some suggestions:

❖ Face the speaker
❖ Maintain eye contact
❖ Minimise external distractions (for example, having the TV on in the corner of the room)
❖ Respond appropriately
❖ Focus solely on what the speaker is saying and not on what you are going to say next
❖ Keep an open mind
❖ Give positive feedback

Listed below are some additional pointers that help the listening process.

Language

1. Use language appropriate to the age of the children—neither too complex nor too simple.
2. Talk to children as you would to other adults; if you give them value and respect, they will reciprocate.
3. Never assume that you are all-knowing and that they are there to learn. It is more than likely that you will have a lot to learn from them.
4. Check that they understand what you say and are happy with it. Check with them that you have understood what they have been trying to say.
5. If you say something that is wrong, apologise.

Body language

1. Be aware of your body language.
2. Come down to the children's level.
3. Do not use your physical size to intimidate them.
4. Use an open, positive stance—no closed positions, such as folded arms.
5. Maintain eye contact; if you are not looking at the child, you are not listening.

Use of voice

1. Use a quiet voice: children will respond better to a softly spoken person than to one who shouts.
2. Be aware of local accents and phrases that you or they may not understand.
3. Remember that God has given us two ears and only one mouth—so we should listen more than we speak.

Pastoral issues: Children dealing with loss _____

When there is a death, separation, divorce or significant change or upheaval in the family, children have a right to pastoral care. Most children do not need therapeutic intervention in such circumstances. Like most of us, they simply need the loving attention of adults who are eager to connect with them, acknowledge what has happened, understand their pain and encourage the expression of feelings. All changes, large and small, carry with them a sense of loss, and children deserve to get whatever pastoral attention they need to cope with loss and grief.

Children's understanding of death depends upon their age, personality and life experience. Until the age of seven or so, they cannot fully grasp that death is permanent and they may believe that the dead person might return. Often, too, there is a fear that any other separation could be a forerunner of death. Small children are likely to feel frightened and insecure, voicing many questions over and over again. Reassurance and patience are needed in answering questions honestly, acknowledging that we don't know all the answers.

Most children over seven years of age understand that death is permanent and happens to everyone. They need to be reassured that they were not responsible for the death. Sometimes they even deny that it has happened. It is helpful for them to reminisce, maybe by looking at photographs and mementos.

Key points

❖ Remember that when a family is grieving, small acts of kindness mean a great deal.
❖ Acknowledge that children grieve.
❖ Children need to know that it is OK to have all sorts of strong feelings, and that these feelings might last for a while.
❖ Reassure children that they are in no way to blame for the loss.
❖ Give plenty of affection (as appropriate) to reassure children that they are cared about.
❖ Never assume that you know what they are feeling: ask them.
❖ Recognise that children have pastoral care to offer as well as receive.

Share responses to this section, being sensitive to each other's experiences.

Children dealing with bullying ___

Bullying is behaviour 'by an individual or group, usually repeated over time, that intentionally hurts another individual or group either physically or emotionally' (*Safe to Learn*, Department for Children, Schools and Families, 2007).

Bullying involves an imbalance of power. It can be carried out physically, verbally, emotionally or through cyberspace. Children can bully each other, be bullied by adults and, sometimes, bully adults.

There are three widely acknowledged means of bullying:

❖ **direct physical bullying** (pushing, hitting, punching, kicking)
❖ **direct verbal bullying** (yelling abuse at another, name-calling, insulting someone, using verbal threats)
❖ **indirect bullying**, also known as social bullying or relational bullying (spreading rumours, social exclusion, disclosing another's secrets to a third party).

Most major denominations have counter-bullying policies. It is essential that children's leaders make sure everyone understands that bullying of any kind is unacceptable. If it does occur, adults and children should know who they can talk to and be assured that they will be supported. Those who bully need to be helped to understand how they can change the way they behave.

Discuss how you might recognise if a member of your group is being bullied.

Being safe

Any premises in which an activity with children takes place should be physically safe and secure. It is the responsibility of your Christian community to ensure this, and one way of doing it is through risk assessments.

Risk assessments are a proactive approach to lessening the chance that an unexpected event will ever happen, and are used to identify possible problems and situations that could cause harm. They identify objects or activities that could cause harm and evaluate the associated risk, which is a combination of the likelihood of the hazard being realised and the severity of its outcome. Armed with this information, decisions can be made on how the risk is to be controlled.

Adopting a risk assessment approach for the premises in which you meet is good practice. It ensures that conditions are safe and that, so far as is reasonably practical, everything possible has been done to minimise the risk of danger. As a children's worker, you have a responsibility to be aware of what your Christian community has done in this area and, if possible, to review written documentation specific to your premises.

Check the risk assessments that you already have in place and review whether they need to be updated.

Biblical thought

> **You will need:**
> ✳ Photographs of children (cut from newspapers and magazines) showing different ages/races/abilities, different contexts, different emotions and/or postcards collected from art galleries, commercial sets from publishers and greetings cards

Pass round a selection of pictures of children. Reflect on them and how God loves us all without prejudice.

Children are offered as a model of God's being. Share the following biblical insights and/or participants' own suggestions.

❖ A child, Samuel, is the one who hears God speak and then shares a tough message with an adult who will not be glad to hear it (1 Samuel 3:1–18).
❖ A child, Miriam, spots an opportunity, copes in a sensitive way and changes history. Missing a child's contribution may mean missing a moment of enrichment in our relationship with God (Exodus 1:22—2:10).

As a group, recall moments when a child's insight enriched a group or individual.

Take the usual care needed when sharing personal observations and, if appropriate, discuss the requirements of sensitivity and confidentiality in talking about individual children.

Reflection on learning

Adults are told to show Christ-like attention to children by providing for their physical, spiritual and emotional needs: not offering a stone instead of bread; not placing stumbling blocks in their way; not provoking them by unreasonable behaviour (Matthew 7:7–11; Mark 9:42; Ephesians 6:4).

❖ Share what you have learnt from the session and what action you need to take.
❖ Identify the key people who have responsibility for your church or organisation, and plan to ask them what they think about the pastoral awareness issues raised in this session.

Worship

God listens very carefully to what children say. In fact, God gives full attention to every word we all say. God loves you wholeheartedly, and whatever is important to you is important to God.

In John 6:1–13, adults, children and young people share together in feeding five thousand people, when the apparently minuscule and laughably ridiculous offering of a child contributes to the transformation of a difficult situation.

Prayer of St Patrick's Breastplate

All: Christ be with me, Christ within me,
Christ behind me, Christ before me,
Christ beside me, Christ to win me,
Christ to comfort and restore me,
Christ beneath me, Christ above me,
Christ in quiet, Christ in danger,
Christ in hearts of all that love me,
Christ in mouth of friend and stranger.

Leader: May Christ be in all our work with children, giving us wisdom to listen and eyes to see when something is wrong. Amen

Suggested song

Take this moment (*Wild Goose Songs* Vol. 3, Wild Goose Publications)

Misuse of power in worship

The following is a list of suggested examples of bad practice concerning worship with children. Do you agree with those chosen? Talk together about times when you have witnessed these things happening in church. What else might you like to add to this list? How might you go about challenging church practice in this area?

❖ They are 'picked on' to answer a question.

❖ They are made to feel foolish because of their lack of knowledge.

❖ They are used as token participants ('hold this'; 'be the butt of a joke'; 'accessorise me').

❖ They are used to read something that someone else has written or decided is suitable.

❖ They are only invited to respond to closed questions with 'right' answers.

❖ Their opinions and ideas are not sought.

❖ They are allocated sound effect noises and gimmick involvement.

❖ They are patronised.

❖ Their trust is manipulated for the entertainment of others.

❖ They are clapped after a contribution, but no one else is applauded.

❖ They are instructed in performing an item without consultation or explanation.

❖ They are viewed as recipients of entertainment designed to keep them 'being good' and 'sitting still'.

❖ They are told the 'right' interpretation of scripture as perceived by the adults.

❖ Their vulnerability is exploited for the benefit of adults.

❖ Their concerns are ignored in the intercessions and other parts of the worship.

Reproduced with permission from *Core Skills for Children's Work* (Barnabas for Children, 2013) **www.barnabasinchurches.org.uk**

The basics for a positive session with children

By our own behaviour we offer our best and live up to our calling. Children need:

❖ **to know they are welcome:** They are greeted genuinely by name and they are encouraged to greet all others in the learning community.

❖ **to see that their place is ready:** The meeting place is comfortable and attractively prepared and there are things to do from the moment they arrive.

❖ **to be safe:** There are no hazards in the room and any 'community rules' are known and understood by all.

❖ **to have your attention:** Everything is prepared, the running order is planned, and the children are the focus for the time you have together.

❖ **to experience your skills:** You have practised your method and the whole team is fully briefed.

❖ **to have quality resources:** The church budget covers children's ministry and enables you to offer the best in all aspects of your programme.

❖ **to have your prayers:** Leaders spend time praying regularly about children and know their situations.

❖ **to have your interest:** You remember previous conversations; you listen; you observe.

❖ **to be encouraged:** Time is given for thought when questions are posed, and answers are appropriately affirmed.

❖ **to know the boundaries:** It is clear what is expected of them, because a consistent approach is offered.

❖ **to be engaged:** Activities are designed with their abilities in mind, and a variety of approaches are used to ensure that all can participate.

❖ **to know, by your attitude, God's love:** You see them as precious, and understand that it is your privilege to be with them.

Reproduced with permission from *Core Skills for Children's Work* (Barnabas for Children, 2013) **www.barnabasinchurches.org.uk**

Personal reflection sheet

What did you learn from this session?

How will this affect the way you work with children?

What further items in this area would you like to follow up?

Reproduced with permission from *Core Skills for Children's Work* (Barnabas for Children, 2013) **www.barnabasinchurches.org.uk**

CORE SESSION 5: PASTORAL AWARENESS **67**

Portfolio checklist

Learning outcomes

❖ To share insights about a variety of pastoral issues.
❖ To explore how power is used in working with children.
❖ To identify issues involved in providing a safe environment for children, physically, emotionally and spiritually.

To show that the learning outcomes have been achieved, your portfolio must include at least the following. *(Tick when you have included each one in the file.)*

☐ Personal reflection sheet

☐ Notes you have taken during CORE Session 5, with any additional ideas

☐ A copy of your policy statement for child protection

☐ A reflection about the building where you work with children

☐ Any other responses or reflections you wish to include

The participant's involvement in a group for CORE Session 5, 'Pastoral awareness', is confirmed. The learning outcomes have been achieved through the evidence provided.

Signed (assessor)_____ Date _____

Any comments from assessor

Signed (candidate)_____ Date _____

CORE SESSION SIX
The Bible and prayer

Aim

To explore ways of handling Bible stories and encouraging prayer with children.

Learning outcomes

❖ To explore ways of nurturing the innate spirituality of children.
❖ To gain an understanding of how Bible stories can enrich prayer and faith development.
❖ To experience a time of prayer and reflection.
❖ To develop an awareness of the different styles of prayer that may be used, both in community worship activities and in personal communication with God.
❖ To introduce different ways of working with Bible stories creatively.

Materials needed

Starters

❖ Some lightweight, stackable chairs
❖ Bibles

Core

❖ Several photocopies (on card if possible) of the quotations and Bible verses on page 74. Cut each page into individual cards, allowing one complete set for every two or three people.
❖ Bibles
❖ Four tables with a few chairs around them
❖ A copy of the four cards on the 'Using the Bible' activity sheet (see page 75)
❖ At least four modern translations of the Bible
❖ Plain paper, pencils, crayons
❖ A bowl or jar of assorted threadable beads (find old necklaces or similar in charity shops)
❖ Some balls of thin wool or thread
❖ Scissors
❖ Sticky notes
❖ Four small cards, each with one of the following Bible references written on it: James 1:2–4; Romans 15:7; Colossians 1:9–14; Colossians 2:6–7
❖ A large lighted candle (make sure it is safe)
❖ Enough tealights for everyone
❖ Reflective music

Worship

❖ Copies of the 'Bible images' pictures on page 76
❖ A Bible

Opening thought

One day Jesus was praying in a certain place. When he had finished, one of his disciples said to him, 'Lord, teach us to pray, just as John taught his disciples.'
Luke 11:1 (GNB)

Starters

What's so special about the Bible?

> **You will need:**
> * A Bible

The following icebreaker activity is an adaptation of a party game that could lead into a short discussion about the different Christian understandings of the Bible. You will need one Bible.

Sit the group in a circle facing inwards. A leader should introduce the Bible with the formula 'This is a Bible and it is…', adding his or her own favourite description or definition, such as 'a book of amazing stories' or 'a very long history book' or 'a collection of stories about God'.

Then the person to the left should take the same Bible, repeat the first person's description and add one of their own. Each time the Bible is passed on, the person receiving the Bible should repeat everything that has been said before and add a new definition. This continues round the circle, with the ways of describing the Bible growing each time.

Which definitions were variations on a theme and which were surprising? This could lead into a short discussion on how Christians view their special book.

Can the group think of any more unusual descriptions of the Bible?

Passing on the Bible

> **You will need:**
> * Two Bibles

The Bible has been faithfully passed down through the generations. In our turn we are called to pass on what we have received, so that the next generation can hear for themselves the story of God's love for the world. This icebreaker game picks up on this idea and could be a way into a session on how we can pass the Bible story on in our day.

Ask the group to stand in a well-spaced circle. Explain that they will need to use their imaginations as they take part in a Bible relay race. The aim is to think up as many different ways as possible that they can 'pass the Bible on' to the next person in the circle.

Give examples of what is meant, such as passing the Bible on 'furtively' (hide it under your jumper and look around nervously) or 'enthusiastically' (pass it on with a flourish and a jump).

Give the group a short while to think of different ways that they could pass the Bible 'baton' on in this game. The 'handovers' should be different each time. This will get harder toward the second half of the Bible's journey around the circle.

Afterwards, reflect together on how the Bible was passed on. Was it only as a closed book? Reluctantly or with conviction? Deliberately or by accident? With embarrassment or with passion? With words or in silence? Acrobatically or sheepishly? Perhaps the group could manage a second relay round, with some new types of passing on.

End this icebreaker with a reading from Psalm 78:1–8, which talks about how we have a story to pass on to the next generation, so that our children and those not yet born will, in their time, come to put their trust in God.

What is prayer?

> **You will need:**
> * Some lightweight, stackable chairs

Divide into groups of two or three and give each group two chairs. Invite them to decide on how many different ways they can arrange the chairs so that they are somehow linked or connected (for example, facing each other, on top of each other, behind each other, one upside down in front of the other, and so on).

What do the different ways of arranging the chairs tell us about the different connections or 'conversations' that could be taking place between people on the two chairs?

Link this idea to prayer. How do we sit down with God? Side by side? Opposite each other? In his arms?

Prompt more thoughts about prayer with the following questions:

❖ I wonder if there is any one way of talking with God that is best.
❖ I wonder how God wants to sit down with us.
❖ I wonder if different ways of sitting or arranging ourselves are linked to different sorts of conversations with God.
❖ I wonder if having an empty chair nearby might help us pray.
❖ I wonder which arrangement for prayer you like best.

CORE

Children and spirituality

> You will need:
> ✳ Several photocopies (on card if possible) of the quotations and Bible verses relating to children's spirituality on page 74). Cut each page into individual cards, allowing one complete set for every two or three people.

Divide into groups of two or three, each having a set of the cards to read and talk about together. What are the similarities between the quotations? What are the differences? Which do you like? With which do you disagree?

What do these quotes tell us about children's spirituality and spirituality in general?

Exploring the Bible creatively

There are many ways of exploring the Bible creatively. Usually, when we are with children, we tend to read or tell stories and ask the children to look for information, rather than helping them to listen and find meanings for themselves in what they read. Reading or hearing scripture should be a spiritual experience, not just a fact-finding activity. It is one of the ways in which we can meet with God. The stories are important, but children also need to be given the freedom to think for themselves and relate what they hear to their own lives. They are the only ones who can do that. They are the real experts on their own lives and on their own relationship with God.

It is more helpful to discuss the stories with the children than simply to ask a range of 'right or wrong' questions. This emphasises the fact that we don't have the only answers, and that our relationship with the story is more important than factual recall. It is more important for children to hear the stories and respond than to remember the details. If they have experienced the story themselves in some way, they are more likely to remember it.

It is not helpful to tell the children what the story 'means' or to impose our own understanding of the story on them. As Jesus encouraged his listeners to discover their own understanding of his parables, so children's workers can allow their listeners to interpret stories in their own way.

In small groups, discuss how you feel about this attitude to using the Bible with children.

✳ Does it make you feel uneasy because you think you ought to have all the right answers?
✳ Or does it feel better to know that you are not expected to know everything?
✳ Do you feel comfortable with the idea that children can think things through with you?
✳ Do you think that you could learn anything from the children about the Bible stories you share with them?

How many ways can you tell a Bible story?

> You will need:
> ✳ Bibles

In small groups, choose a Bible story and decide which methods you could use to tell the story to children. Here are some ideas that you can add to those suggested by the group.

✤ Tell it from memory
✤ Put it in your own words
✤ Make a BIG picture (a mural, or life-size)
✤ Banners
✤ Little pictures
✤ Individual pictures
✤ A video film
✤ Rap it
✤ Ask people questions that will lead them to tell the story
✤ Tell it with sound effects
✤ Visual aids
✤ Story coat (a coat with pictures and artefacts that tell or remind us of the story)
✤ Audience participation
✤ Masks
✤ Cartoons
✤ Songs (songs you know, or making up new words to old tunes, or old words to new tunes)
✤ Puppets (stick, glove, marionettes, paper cut-outs, dancing dolls)
✤ Taking visual aids out of a special bag
✤ Mime
✤ Dance
✤ Dressing-up box drama
✤ Poetry
✤ Improvise a drama
✤ Narrator tells while actors act (or all do actions)

Using the Bible

> **You will need:**
> * Four tables with a few chairs around them
> * A copy of the four cards on the 'Using the Bible' activity sheet (see page 75)
> * At least four modern translations of the Bible
> * Plain paper, pencils, crayons
> * A bowl or jar of assorted (threadable) beads
> * Some balls of thin wool or thread
> * Scissors
> * Sticky notes
> * Four small cards, each with one of the following Bible references written on it: James 1:2–4; Romans 15:7; Colossians 1:9–14; Colossians 2:6–7
> * A large lighted candle
> * Enough tealights for everyone
> * Reflective music

Preparation

Set out the four tables (to be designated 'Praise', 'Letters', 'Questions' and 'A story about Jesus') and some chairs, one table in each corner of the room. On each table, place one or two modern translations of the Bible, some plain paper, pencils, crayons and a copy of the appropriate card from the 'Using the Bible' activity sheet on page 75.

On the 'Praise' table, add the bowl or jar of beads, the balls of thin wool or thread, and scissors.

On the 'Letters' table, add the four small cards showing the Bible references James 1:2–4, Romans 15:7, Colossians 1:9–14 and Colossians 2:6–7.

On the 'Questions' table, add the large, lighted candle and enough tealights for everyone.

Nothing extra is required for the 'A story about Jesus' table.

Method

Divide into four groups to visit a table each and to follow the instructions on the cards. If there is time, a group could visit more than one table. Allow about 25 minutes for this activity, including time at the end for people to share their experiences of the task.

During this exercise, you might like to play some quiet, restful music and place some chairs away from the tables in case anyone wants to be on their own for a while.

Prayer

Prayer is an expression of a growing relationship with God. Christians focus their prayers on God through Jesus.

Prayer can take many forms: some people prefer formal prayers; others are happier with unspoken words. When we are working with children, it is possible that we will encourage them to use the prayer styles with which *we* are most comfortable, rather than helping them to discover other ways of communicating with God. Those ways might include:

* **Meditative prayer:** Reading a Bible verse or passage to help focus on God.
* **Liturgical prayer:** Repeating or reading a prayer that has been written or taught by someone else.
* **Active prayer:** Praying while walking or moving or doing something.
* **Shared prayers:** Praying aloud with others in small or large groups.
* **Conversational prayer:** Speaking to God in a conversational way, listening for answers as well as telling God our thoughts.
* **Spontaneous or 'arrow' prayers:** An immediate response to something that is happening.

As a group, use the following questions to prompt discussion:

* How were you taught to pray?
* Has your preferred style of prayer changed over the years?
* Is there a difference between the way you pray privately and the way you pray in public?
* How do you encourage children to pray?

Creative prayer ideas

In small groups, come up with as many creative ways of praying as you can. Here are some ideas that you can add to those suggested by the group.

* Something to look at or hold
* Using tealights or candles
* A holding cross
* Using a globe
* Rolling dice (1=me, 2=parents, 3=family, 4=friends, 5=church, 6=world)
* Prayer tree
* Using pictures
* Action prayers
* Finger prayers
* Sign language
* Facing different directions
* Simple rhyming prayers
* Prayer stations
* Labyrinths
* Sand trays
* Lava lamps

- ❖ Blowing bubbles
- ❖ Unknotting ropes
- ❖ Sticky notes
- ❖ Patterns (for example, TSP = Thank you, Sorry, Please; STOP = Sorry, Thank you, Others, Praise)

Now think of your work with children. Consider which new styles of prayer you could try together.

Biblical thought

Jesus often taught with stories and illustrations that left people to work out meanings for themselves. Maybe that would mean taking time to ponder alone or maybe talking it over with friends. New insights could dawn, or old things could be seen in new ways.

Once, Jesus asked the disciples whether they understood all the things he had been telling them. When they said 'Yes', he went on to explain that becoming a disciple is like being 'the owner of a house who brings out of the storeroom new treasures as well as old' (Matthew 13:51–52, NIV).

Reflection on learning

Looking back over the activities in this session:

- ❖ What encouragements, concerns and challenges has this module raised for you?
- ❖ Is there something from this session that could also benefit the wider church community?
- ❖ Which aspects of this session might you talk about and check out with the children in your group?

Worship

> You will need:
> ✳ Copies of the 'Bible images' activity sheet pictures on page 76
> ✳ A Bible

Reflect together on how the Bible and prayer relate to these pictures.

Prayers

Use the pictures as a way to pray for inspiration for each other in your work with children.

Suggested songs

The word of the Lord is planted in my heart (*Kidsource*, Kevin Mayhew)
I want to walk with Jesus Christ (*Mission Praise*, Marshall Pickering)
Make the book live to me (*Junior Praise*)
Kum ba yah, my Lord (Traditional)

The soul is healed by being with children. English proverb	Don't limit a child to your own learning, for he was born in another time. Rabbinical saying
Right from the beginning [the child] is already in possession of that value and those depths which are implied in the name of a person. It is not simply that he gradually grows into a person. He is a person… The child is the person who, right from the first, is the partner of God. Karl Rahner, *Ideas for a Theology of Childhood*	Children are not colouring books. You don't get to fill them in with your favourite colours. Khaled Hosseini, *The Kite Runner*
Children should be helped to develop the spiritual qualities of wonder and inner peace— and the sense of something greater than themselves… No child is complete without some passionate spiritual engagement of this kind. Richard Layard & Judy Dunn, *A Good Childhood*	Children… have spiritual abilities that defy conventional chronological categories of faith development. Religious faith does not develop in quite the same way as other parts of our bodies and minds from small to large or from immature to mature. Growing up, in fact, does not guarantee spiritual development. Bonnie J. Miller-McLemore, *Let the Children Come*
Our birth is but a sleep and a forgetting: *The soul that rises with us, our life's star,* *Hath had elsewhere its setting,* *And cometh from afar.* *Not in entire forgetfulness…* *But trailing clouds of glory, do we come* *From God, who is our home:* *Heaven lies about us in our infancy.* William Wordsworth, from 'Intimations of Immortality'	*Your children are not your children.* *They are the sons and daughters of Life's longing for itself.* *They come through you but not from you…* *For their souls dwell in the house of tomorrow,* *which you cannot visit, not even in your dreams.* *You may strive to be like them,* *but seek not to make them like you.* Kahlil Gibran, 'On children'
Children may be the model for adult spiritual development, rather than the reverse… A task for adult spiritual development may be to recapture the child's more inclusive and all-pervading sense of relation to the spiritual, which means for them it is normally 'everyday' rather than dramatic. Rebecca Nye, *Children's Spirituality*	Many see playing as a superficial or trivial act, but I see it as a life-giving act. It makes us young when we are old and matures us when we are young. Jerome Berryman, *Godly Play*
With praises from children and from tiny infants, you have built a fortress. It makes your enemies silent, and all who turn against you are left speechless. Psalm 8:2	'See that you do not despise one of these little ones. For I tell you that their angels in heaven always see the face of my Father in heaven.' Matthew 18:10 (NIV)

Reproduced with permission from *Core Skills for Children's Work* (Barnabas for Children, 2013) **www.barnabasinchurches.org.uk**

Praise

Read a psalm marked as a psalm of praise in the Bible (for example, Psalm 8, Psalm 27 or Psalm 100) and think about all the things the writer is thanking God for. Are they things that make you want to praise God? What would you like to thank God for?

As a group, think about all the things in your lives that remind you of God's love. Thread a bead on to the wool for each of these things. Perhaps you could choose a bead that reminds you in some way of the thing you are saying 'thank you' for. While you thread the beads, thank God for all these blessings.

Letters

Choose one of the following Bible references and find the verses in a Bible: James 1:2–4; Romans 15:7; Colossians 1:9–14; Colossians 2:6–7. They are all taken from the letters written to new churches soon after Jesus' life on earth. The writer (either Paul or James) is helping the new churches to live out their faith and to be good witnesses to the difference that Jesus has made to their lives. He is encouraging to the new Christians but he is honest as well, and sometimes sounds quite severe.

Imagine he has written these words to you and your church. Read the passage and discuss in your group how it might relate to you. What is God saying to you through this letter? Write a quick reply on a sticky note, from the group to Paul or James.

Questions

Think of some of the parts of the Bible that people find difficult (for example, suffering as described in Job, judgments such as the ten plagues in Exodus, or genocide as in Joshua). They may be difficult because they are hard to understand or because they say things that we don't really want to hear. Sometimes passages in the Bible seem to ask us questions more than they give us answers. Think of something that puzzles you about what the Bible says, and concentrate on this issue. We may not know the answer or explanation for a very long time.

Light a tealight from a larger candle for each difficult question you have been thinking about.

A story about Jesus

Choose one of the following stories about Jesus: the storm at sea (Luke 8:22–25); the feeding of the 5000 (John 6:1–15); Jesus and the woman who anoints his feet with perfume (Mark 14:3–9). Imagine yourself there in the scene while it is happening. In your imagination, let the story unfold as if you were watching a movie. Now, as a group, share your responses to this exercise. What can you see, hear, smell or touch? Who else is there? What emotions are you experiencing?

Together, create a piece of word art that captures how everybody felt about the story.

Reproduced with permission from *Core Skills for Children's Work* (Barnabas for Children, 2013) www.barnabasinchurches.org.uk

CORE SESSION 6: THE BIBLE AND PRAYER **75**

Personal reflection sheet

What did you learn from this session?

How will this affect the way you work with children?

What further items in this area would you like to follow up?

Reproduced with permission from *Core Skills for Children's Work* (Barnabas for Children, 2013) www.barnabasinchurches.org.uk

Portfolio checklist

Learning outcomes

✤ To explore ways of nurturing the innate spirituality of children.
✤ To gain an understanding of the ways in which Bible stories can enrich prayer and faith development.
✤ To experience a time of prayer and reflection.
✤ To develop an awareness of the different styles of prayer that may be used, both in community worship activities and in personal communication with God.
✤ To introduce different ways of working with Bible stories creatively.

To show that the learning outcomes have been achieved, your portfolio must include at least the following. (*Tick when you have included each one in the file.*)

☐ Personal reflection sheet

☐ Notes from the starter activity

☐ Your views on using Bible stories with children

☐ A record of how you might tell Bible stories to children in a variety of ways

☐ Examples of how you have prayed with children in two different ways

☐ A brief account of a personal experience of spiritual reflection

☐ Any other responses or reflections you wish to include

☐ The participant's involvement in a group for CORE Session 6, 'The Bible and prayer', is confirmed. The learning outcomes have been achieved through the evidence provided.

Signed (assessor)_____ Date _____

Any comments from assessor

Signed (candidate)_____ Date _____

Reproduced with permission from *Core Skills for Children's Work* (Barnabas for Children, 2013) **www.barnabasinchurches.org.uk**

78 CORE SKILLS

Bibliography

Consultative Group on Ministry among Children, *The Child in the Church*, British Council of Churches, 1976

Consultative Group on Ministry among Children, *Unfinished Business*, CCBI, 1991

John Henson, *Good as New: A radical retelling of the scriptures*, O Books, 2004

Leslie Francis, *Urban Hope and Spiritual Health*, Epworth, 2006

Francis Bridger, *Children Finding Faith*, SU, 2003

Marcia Bunge, *The Child in Christian Thought*, Eerdmans, 2001

Kathleen Marshall and Paul Parvis, *Honouring Children*, St Andrews Press, 2004

Judith Wigley, *Working with Under 5s*, SU, 2005

Claire Saunders and Hilary Porritt, *Working with 8–10s*, SU, 2005

Tricia Williams and John Stephenson, *Working with 11–14s*, SU, 2005

Jerome Berryman, *Teaching Godly Play*, Send the Good News, 2009

General Synod Board of Education, *Sharing the Good News with Children*, CHP, 2003

Keith J. White, *The Growth of Love*, BRF, 2008

Rebecca Nye, *Children's Spirituality*, Church House Press, 2010

David Hay and Rebecca Nye, *The Spirit of the Child*, Jessica Kingsley, 2006

Gretchen Wolff Pritchard, *Offering the Gospel to Children*, Cowley, 1992

Craig Jutila, *Leadership Essentials for Children's Ministry*, Group Publishing, 2002

Catherine Stonehouse and Scottie May, *Listening to Children on the Spiritual Journey*, Baker Academic, 2010

Michael Yaconelli, *Dangerous Wonder*, Navpress, 1998

Roots for Churches: Worship and Learning for the Whole Church, MPH, bi-monthly

Light: Bible-based learning resources for all ages, SU

International Journal of Children's Spirituality, IACS

Simon Bass, *Special Children Special Needs*, CHP, 2003

Wendy Duffy, *Children and Bereavement*, CHP, 2003

Wholly Worship Too, URC, 2000

Charter for Children in the Church, URC, 2004

Will Our Children Have Faith? John Westerhoff III, Morehouse, 2012

Richard Layard and Judy Dunn, *A Good Childhood: Searching for values in a competitive age*, Penguin, 2009

Glenn Miles and Josephine-Joy Wright (eds.), *Celebrating Children*, Paternoster, 2001

Ivy Beckworth, *Postmodern Children's Ministry*, Zondervan, 2004

Jerome Berryman, *Children and the Theologians*, Morehouse, 2009

Anne Richards and Peter Privet (eds.), *Through the Eyes of a Child*, Church House Publishing, 2009